KNOW YOUR BIBLE SERIES

4

SAMUEL
KINGS
JOSHUA
JUDGES
EZEKIEL
SECOND ISAIAH

ROY L. SMITH

ABINGDON PRESS
NASHVILLE

Samuel, Kings, Joshua, Judges, Ezekiel, Second Isaiah

No. 209153

Printed in U.S.A.

INTRODUCTION

A generation that reads about deportations, governments in exile, refugees, demolished cities, forced labor, and puppet princes, in every morning's newspapers, should find the study of the problems and sufferings of the Jews in their Babylonian exile very modern. Caught as they were in a vortex of world upheaval, and becoming victims of a powerful and ruthless overlord determined on world mastery, the records of the spiritual struggles of the Jewish people should be thrilling for modern readers.

It is one of the unfortunate results of superficial Bible-study methods that the very great spiritual achievements of the Jews during the period of their Babylonian exile are almost entirely unknown to the modern Christian. The very fact that the books of Samuel and of Kings appear in the fore part of the Bible gives the uninstructed reader the impression that they are records which antedate the prophets by many centuries. Many have never heard that these writings were originally religious tracts written for the purpose of inspiring loyalty to Yahweh in the midst of conditions that were extremely discouraging.

The mysterious symbolism of Ezekiel has been so confusing to the average reader that he has given up in despair, not realizing that he has before his eyes a human document of very great interest. The accident that linked probably two books of prophetical writings with the name of Isaiah has beclouded the majestic heights to which adventurous spirits of the Exile undertook to lead the people. The result is that we have never fully appreciated the great truths found in those sublime poems.

Great adventure awaits the devout student who sets out to discover the literature of the Exile. If he is spiritually sensitive he will be profoundly moved by the despair that steeled down upon the people who had found the earth suddenly going out from under them, and he will stand reverently in the presence of those heroes of the faith who lifted up the soul of the nation in that supreme hour of trial. He will come to appreciate the determined wistfulness with which the people continued to sing the songs of Zion in a strange land.

If may require a bit of holy imagination to see the faith of those who found room, somewhere in the bundles of baggage which they shouldered for hundreds of miles across the hot sands, for the precious rolls whereon were recorded the great names and the prophetic faith of their people. But to those pious ones who left something precious behind in order that the rolls might go into Exile with the people, in Babylonia to become the inspiration for the faith and the basis for the Scriptures of the new Israel, the modern Christian owes a debt he will never be able to pay. He who can look upon that caravan of struggling captives, bending under their burdens and carrying the sacred rolls in addition to their food and clothing, and not be moved to the depths of his being is slow of heart indeed.

It may be something of a surprise to some who have been reared in the traditional concept of the Scriptures to discover that they are, after all, very human and down to earth. As we first encounter the evidence that the writings of more than one prophet are included in the book we call Isaiah it may prove disquieting. But as we seek further and discover the spiritual magnitude of the great prophet of the Exile we will be content to allow him to go nameless, and be thankful for the vision and courage he inspires in us. As we gather the facts and look the evidence in face we will discover that our Bible has suddenly become greater and more awesome than ever, even though our preconceptions have been somewhat altered. No truth is ever lost because new facts are discovered, though we may be compelled to rearrange our opinions.

Roy L. Smith

Refugees Who Wrote Scripture

1 Who were the refugees?

The years between 597 B.C., when the first Hebrews were led out of Judah into the captivity of Babylonia, and 536 B.C., when the first permission was given for some of them to return to their ancestral land, are known to students of Bible history as the period of the Babylonian Exile. They constitute, so far as the Bible is concerned, a span of years extremely significant. It was during this period that a group of books came into their present form as a result of the literary and religious activity of the Hebrew exiles who had been deported to Babylonia. There can be no real understanding of the Old Testament without some knowledge of the fundamental changes that took place in them and in their faith during those years.

2 Why are the Hebrews called Jews?

Up to the time of the Babylonian exile the Hebrews were called the Children of Israel. But with the destruction of Samaria (721 B.C.), and the disappearance of the northern kingdom of Israel, the destiny of the race rested with the small southern kingdom of Judah. The captives who were carried off to Babylonia were first called "Judeans" by their captors and in time this was shortened to "Jews," somewhat as the name "Yankees" has been shortened to "Yanks." One of the surprising facts about the nickname is that the Hebrews themselves adopted it, much as the Methodists adopted a nickname as their official title. This change of name is only one of many alterations brought about by the Exile.

3 How did the Exile come about?

From the year 734 B.C., when Ahaz, king of Judah, put his little kingdom under the "protection" of Assyria at the time of the threat from Israel and Syria (II Kings 16:5-20), until the city of Nineveh fell in 612 B.C., bringing the overlordship of the

Assyrian Empire to an end, Judah existed only by the sufferance of the Assyrian monarchs and by the payment of an annual tribute which left the people pauper poor. It was the Assyrian policy to take the last sack of grain, the last cruse of oil, and the last skin of wine that could be extracted from a subject land, and under this program an aristocracy of pagan landlords and money-lenders had grown up in Jerusalem which manipulated the government and passed the burden of taxes on to the people.

In the confusion that followed the fall of Nineveh in 612 B.C., and the rise of the new Babylonian Empire (sometimes called Chaldea), Egypt busied herself in an effort to create strong protective barriers between herself and Babylonia, and in this she proposed that Judah should play a conspicuous part. This led to a desperate battle between the giant powers at Carchemish in 605 B.C., in which the Babylonians were victorious and the mastery of the East passed into the hands of Nebuchadrezzar, the Babylonian king. Thereafter the trains of tribute were driven northeast instead of southwest.

In the midst of these critical events a citizen-clique—"a people's party"—seized control of the government at Jerusalem. The leaders had little knowledge of world politics, and less knowledge of the terrible striking power of the new kingdom of Babylonia. Under pressure from the farmers, who had always borne the major portion of the burden of the tribute, Jehoiakim, the king, raised the standard of revolt and struck out against Babylonia in a vain bid for independence.

Nebuchadrezzar, emperor of Babylonia, was occupied with other matters for the moment and made no move against the rebels, but was content to allow the desert tribes, who nursed ancient grudges against the Hebrews, to pillage the homes and villages of the Judeans (II Kings 24:1-2). As soon as he found it convenient, however, the king took matters into his own hands and came thundering down upon the little kingdom with a huge force. Jeremiah had anticipated this move (8:4—9:22), but his warnings had been ignored.

Jehoiakim died in the midst of the struggle and was succeeded by his son Jehoiachin, a youth only eighteen years of age. Within three months of his accession to the throne the final blow was struck. As the Babylonians came rushing through the gates of the capital, they seized the young king, his mother Nehushta, who was a distinguished woman of the realm, and all the king's wives, carrying them away in a hopeless group to Babylonia as trophies (II Kings 24:8-17). In addition to the royal family, artisans, priests, business leaders, and other leading citizens were deported (II Kings 24:11-17; II Chronicles 36:9-10).

Nebuchadrezzar was not actually desirous of destroying the city of Jerusalem. He would have been quite content to leave the kingdom intact if he could have trusted its government. As proof of his good intent he set up an uncle of Jehoiachin as a puppet and gave him the name of Zedekiah, trusting him with surprisingly large powers (II Kings 24:17-20).

Among those who were left in the land there was a strong pro-Egyptian party, and ambassadors from the Nile were soon able to stir up trouble. Added to this was the very important fact that the king was surrounded by rural landlords who were quite incapable of dealing with a delicate international situation. In spite of the fact that Zedekiah seems to have been a man easily influenced by flattery, he may have been crowded by his henchmen until he raised the standard of revolt. At any rate the city this time was completely destroyed after a seige which, for sheer agony, has few parallels in history. More thousands were deported to Babylonia (II Kings 25:3-21, II Chronicles 36:17 ff.) and the career of Judah came to an end.

4 Were all the people carried away?

The campaign was directed primarily against the city of Jerusalem and the country districts were little disturbed. The Temple treasure—a very valuable bit of loot—was hauled away to Babylon, and a host of skilled workmen were included among the evacuees, for which there is a simple explanation.

5 Why were workmen deported?

The inscriptions which remain to us indicate that during his long reign (605-562 B.C.) Nebuchadrezzar was a famous builder. The kingdom of Babylonia was a comparatively young nation, and during the quarter of a century that it was winning its freedom from Assyria there had been little time for the construction of public works. The military campaigns which had won the victory had cost many lives, and thousands of workmen were needed for the construction of canals, palaces, temples, and cities. Like modern Germany during World War II, Babylonia needed skilled workmen more than acres.

6 How many captives were taken?

The most reliable statistics seem to be found in Jeremiah, who mentions 3,023 deported in 597 B.C., 832 in 586 B.C., and 745 in 582 B.C., making a total of 4,600 (Jeremiah 52:28-30). Many years afterwards the compilers of the book of Kings reported 8,000 in the first deportation (II Kings 24:16), and in another case set the estimate at 10,000 (II Kings 24:14), not including blacksmiths and locksmiths.

7 What happened to the city of Jerusalem?

The Temple and the royal palace were completely destroyed together with all the precious treasures—Temple vessels, bronze pillars, articles of gold being shipped to Babylonia to adorn the temples there. The houses of the rich and noble, after being thoroughly sacked, were raced to the ground. The walls of the city were leveled and everything possible done to wipe the beautiful capital out of existence and leave it a mass of rubble (II Kings 25:9-17).

8 How did the Jews fare in Babylonia?

As Rome ruled the world in Jesus' day, so Babylonia ruled the East at the beginning of the sixth century B.C. Egypt maintained an erratic independence and was able to offer considerable resistance. Other states were in revolt from time to time, but Babylonia ruled the East and, in the main ruled it rather well. Ancient records which have been dug out of the ruins of cities and temples indicate very clearly that a high state of civilization existed in the valley of the Tigris and Euphrates. The Hebrews were installed as captives in the midst of culture, advanced scientific agriculture, brilliant economic adventures, and elaborate political organization.

The city of Babylon, itself, was a very great metropolis. It was surrounded with almost five miles of wall, eighty feet thick and studded with ninety towers. It was a city of magnificent temples and public buildings and was the cultural as well as the political capital of the world. Well-stocked libraries, an abundance of art treasures, and educational opportunities were available. Literature was produced in a variety of forms which included a considerable body of religious material. Wealth abounded and commercial opportunities were numerous and attractive. Trade was the life of the land and physical comforts were to be had in some abundance.

On the whole it may be said the deportees had never lived in such a lovely country in all their lives. They had never seen so much culture; they had never been in contact with so many advantages. In at least two aspects of life they might have considered themselves extremely fortunate: (1) in the easy living made possible by the rich land; (2) in the liberal policy followed by Babylon in dealing with her captives.

9 What about the easy living?

Judah was a barren, sterile, unpromosing land, whose valleys were narrow and whose limestone hills were forbidding in the extreme. Even at best rainfall was uncertain, and the Judean farmer wrested his living out of the land at a great cost.

Babylonia, on the other hand, was a low, level country with rich alluvial soil ready for seeding. The abundant tides of the Tigris and Euphrates rivers were sufficient to provide moisture for even greedy vegetation, and the primitive ingenuity of Babylonian engineers had mastered the problem of irrigation. The whole countryside was crisscrossed by an elaborate system of canals that never ceased to stir the wonder of the desert-dwellers from west of the Jordan. They had never seen ground produce so abundantly (Psalm 137:1).

10 What was Babylonia's policy toward the exiles?

Whereas the Assyrians had deliberately prevented the Israelites from settling in communities of their own, and had scattered them throughout the Empire for the purpose of stamping out their national consciousness, the Babylonians took exactly the opposite course. They encouraged the Jews to settle in colonies and develop their community life. They were permitted to continue their racial and religious customs, speak their own language, perpetuate their own traditions, and conduct their own affairs about as they pleased so long as they did not interfere with the public peace. Thus they were able to benefit in many ways from their residence in Babylon, even though they were regarded as captives.

11 Were they slaves?

They were captives, but they were not slaves. The Hebrews in Egypt in Moses' day had been bondsmen, but the Jews in Babylonia were free men. True, their movements were somewhat limited, their freedom was restricted, and their life was circumscribed; but they were permitted to engage in business if they chose, they might own property, and they enjoyed many citizenship privileges. Some old records recently unearthed describe a Jewish banking firm—Marusha's Sons—which conducted a prosperous business in the city of Nippur, actually in competition with Babylonian firms.

12 How did they benefit from Babylonia?

The Empire had but one purpose in deporting them. It was necessary to break the power of the little nations in the west in order to protect the Empire's border from attack. Had the leaders of Judah been content to be quiet and submissive to Babylonia, the people might not have been disturbed.

Once they were deported, however, the economic needs of the Empire were such that they were dealt with rather generously. Those who were capable of entering government service found occasional opportunity and those who were willing to work were employed at good wages. Those who were interested in the learning of the land were offered abundant opportunity for broadening their knowledge.

There was no restraint upon them as they practiced the rites of their ancient faith (so far as their removal from the Temple permitted). They were encouraged to maintain their family and clan organizations and govern themselves through their duly authorized "elders." They were permitted to speak their own language and were not required to learn the language of the land. Large gatherings were permitted as long as they maintained order, restrained violence, and did not attempt to plot against the government. Taken as a whole, it must be admitted that a very large measure of civil rights were accorded them.

13 **What was the result of this generous treatment?**

Many of the Jews entered heartily into the busy commercial life of the land and began to make money. In this they were encouraged by the government. Others, of an inquiring mind, began to read the Babylonian literature, and much of the native lore and legend became part of the life of the ordinary Jew. Hebrew youths became interested in Babylonian girls, and many mixed marriages were contracted. Babylonian politics interested some and a few actually worked their way into the service of the government (Nehemiah 1:1). The elaborate worship at the temples attracted many who were religiously minded, and the learning, literature, and philosophy found at the libraries fascinated the scholarly.

Life on the whole was so attractive that when permission was given for those to return who might wish to go back to Judah (536 B.C.) only a small percentage were ready to take advantage of the offer. In fact, it took considerable persuasion to enlist a respectable company. In Jesus' day the number of Jews living in Babylonia far exceeded the number living in Palestine, and there were more learning and culture among the Babylonian Jews than among the Palestinians.

14 **Did the Jews really prosper in Babylonia?**

Many of them became wealthy. Some owned great houses and enjoyed lucrative trade with their neighbors. Traders found all doors opened to them. True, they were always a minority group, but they were never the victims of pogroms.

15 **Did they maintain any contact with their homeland?**

In the year 593 B.C., four years after the first deportation, Zedekiah, the king, undertook to improve the relations of Judah with Babylonia (Jeremiah 29:1-3), and in this effort Jeremiah took great interest. He even wrote letters to the exiles, assuring them that he expected they would be the saving remnant and that his hope of the nation's future rested with them. On another occasion he counseled them to settle down in Babylon, make the best of their situation, cultivate the good will of their neighbors, and otherwise improve their lot; for their exile was to last seventy years (two generations; Jeremiah 29). This letter gave great offense among the exiles so much so that a prophet among them replied in vigorous fashion with the demand that the Jerusalem high priest should imprison Jeremiah for so writing (Jeremiah 29:24-28). This indicates that there may have been considerable interchange during the early years at least.

16 Why did the exiles wish to return?

A minority group within the body of exiles, encouraged by the prophecies of Isaiah and Jeremiah, and driven by the passion of patriotism, never abandoned the hope of a return. In spite of the superior economic advantages offered on the level fertile plains of Babylonia, these sturdy patriots turned back wistfully to the rocks and hills of Judah. A few self-appointed prophets went about among the exiles, keeping the national spirit alive, and in at least one instance so aroused the suspicions of the police that they were burned as seditionists (Jeremiah 29:21-22).

17 How was the religion of the Jews maintained?

In the first deportation there were some priests, and these continued their activities as religious leaders, so far as circumstances would permit (Ezekiel 1:1-3). To them must go a large part of the credit for keeping the national faith alive.

18 Why was Babylonia interested in priests?

The Jerusalem priests, because of the Temple revenues, had become a part of the landed aristocracy of Judah. They owned estates, functioned as landlords, controlled considerable revenues, and affiliated with the money-lending class in many intimate ways. When the nation's leaders were taken captive it was certain that some priests would be included in the number.

19 Do we know the names of any such?

We know the name of at least one—Ezekiel. For the purposes of this study we can ignore some very interesting questions that have come to light in recent years concerning the origins of this great book, leaving them to the technical studies of the scholars, and proceed to an investigation of the essential meaning of the writing itself.

20 Was Ezekiel one of the landed priests?

Concerning his economic interests we know nothing. He seems to have had sufficient leisure to permit him to go about his work as a priest without financial worries. Inasmuch as the exiles were deported without their property, however, it is not likely that he would have been able to carry much wealth with him into Babylonia even if he had been rich.

21 How did the religion of the Jews change during the exile?

Up to the time of the Exile every religion in the world had been associated with some government. There was no religion that was independent of all governments. No religion had ever grown up without governmental protection and sponsorship, and no religion had ever survived the destruction of the state under whose auspices it had developed.

In many lands the kings chose the gods for the people, and a god might be forgotten when the king who had raised it up passed off the scene of action. The mortality rate among gods was very high. Any god that could survive the collapse of the state was never imagined. The destruction of Judah would have seemed to imply the destruction of Yahweh, the God of the Hebrews. But instead the period of the Exile saw him come into an entirely new relationnship with the race.

22 How did this come about?

It was a fundamental conviction of the prophets that the misfortunes of the Hebrews were a direct result of their faithlessness. One note had characterized all their preaching—
the nation had sinned and Yahweh was about to punish it.

Different prophets described the nation's sin in different terms, but all agreed on the basic fact. They all taught the moral supremacy of God. As the nation ignored him its fortunes fell; as it obeyed him its fortunes improved.

The Jews in exile, deprived of the services of their beloved Temple and living as aliens in a strange land, were reminded daily of their national humiliation, and they came at last to the solemn conviction that all their troubles rooted back in the fact that they had sinned against God and had not kept his law. In the belief that an accurate and correct observance of their ancient law would open the way for their deliverance, the more pious and patriotic among them turned to a study of the law with a zeal that was almost fanatical.

23 Of what did the law consist?

At first it consisted only of the Book of the Law found in the Temple in 621 B.C. But as the exile wore on and study was given to the matter, the law was elaborated into a complicated system.

24 What books did the Hebrews carry into exile?

The student must keep in mind the fact that the Hebrews produced much more literature than is included in our Old Testament. Some of that material has been lost completely and no mention of it has been made anywhere. On the other hand, mention is made of a number of books, such as "The Book of the Wars of Yahweh" (Numbers 21:14), "The Book of Jashar" (II Samuel 1:18), "A Book of Samuel" (I Samuel 10:25), "The Acts of Solomon" (I Kings 11:41), "The Chronicles of Samuel the Seer" (I Chronicles 29:29), "The Chronicles of Nathan the Prophet" (I Chronicles 29:29), "The Chronicles of Gad the Seer (I Chronicles 29:29), "The Chronicles of Shemaiah" (II Chronicles 12:15), "The Book of the Chronicles of the Kings of Israel" (II Kings 1:18), "The Book of the Chronicles of the Kings of Judah" (II Kings 16:19), "The Prophecy of Ahijah" (II Chronicles 9:29), "The Visions of Iddo" (II Chronicles 9:29), "The Chronicles of the Seers" (II Chronicles 33:19, which included some of the acts of Manasseh), and "The Chronicles of Jehu" (II Chronicles 20:34).

In addition to these which are actually named in the Old Testament, scholars are of the opinion that there were in existence a life of David which is now incorporated into I and II Samuel and some small part of I Kings, a brief life of Isaiah (perhaps a biographical sketch by the prophet himself) which was used in compiling II Kings, probably a small book containing the Elijah stories (I Kings 17; 18; 19; 21 and II Kings 1; 2) and Elisha stories (II Kings 2-8; 13:14-21), and possibly still another which gave an account of the Jehu revolution, in addition to a series of Temple Records (II Kings 9; 19).

Then, of course, there were the prophecies of Amos, Hosea, Isaiah, Micah, Zephaniah, Nahum, Habakkuk, and Jeremiah which were packed away in the baggage. Otherwise they would have perished. From this it is evident that a considerable body of literature went into exile with the people.

25 How important were these books?

The journey was a long and difficult one, and loads were reduced to a minimum. To make more room in the pack for a bulky roll of writing called for devotion of a high order. But there was such among the people; and to those loyal souls among the thousands of evacuees who found room amid their household effects for the precious rolls, the modern Christian owes a debt of gratitude far beyond his power to compute. All this literature was carried on men's backs across hundreds of miles under a burning sun, over roads that tore and wore at the feet of the marchers, by people who were sick at heart, utterly disconsolate, and thoroughly beaten. But on those rolls was recorded in various forms the one thing that was still truly their own—*their faith in Yahweh!*

26 What happened to the land of Judah during the Exile?

It must be remembered that the bulk of the captives were citizens of Jerusalem. Many of the villages and towns were left untouched. But with the Temple in ruins, the government destroyed, and the leading figures in the nation's business, religious and cultural life carried away, there was little left upon which a national life could be rebuilt. The little country town of Mizpah became the capital of the nation (Jeremiah 40; II Kings 25:22-26), but Judah very quickly deteriorated into a helpless colony from which the Babylonians extorted the last possible ounce of tribute. The ruins of Jerusalem housed a few miserables in improvised huts, but the life of the capital had come to an end.

27 What happened to Hebrew religion in Babylonia?

The Exile became a period of very great readjustments in the religious life, practices, and beliefs of the people. There was scarcely a phase of the national religion that did not undergo a profound transformation, with the result that the Jewish religion which came back to the Land of Promise resembled the pre-exilic religion of the Hebrews in some broad general aspects only. Both the fundamental religious thinking of the people, and the mechanics of their worship, were altered very greatly.

28 Who was responsible for this transformation?

A very large number of individuals were concerned with the matter, the vast majority of whom will have to go nameless and unknown. Perhaps it should be said that the final spiritual product was the result of the divine guidance of the nation. But upon the three groups—priests, prophets, scholars—the responsibility rested most heavily.

29 Of what did the transformation consist?

Previous to the Exile all religious thought and worship centered in the Temple at Jerusalem. Here the sin offerings were burned upon the altars; here the favor of Yahweh was besought for the nation. The accuracy with which the forms and ceremonies were performed was a matter of national concern. Everything revolved about the question of national welfare, national safety, and national survival. Men did not offer prayers in behalf of their personal fortunes, and no man thought of his "personal salvation." The idea of personal immortality may have been glimpsed by individuals here and there (II Samuel 12:23), but the doctrine was no part of the nation's religion. Even the great prophets never discussed the question.

In Babylonia, however, the Jews were deprived of all access to their Temple and to the trappings of their religious life, with the result that their faith had to be entirely rebuilt about a new central theme. Their nation was destroyed and through at least the first few years two of their kings were in chains, one of them blinded (Jehoiachin, exiled in 597 B.C., was still alive in 560—II Kings 25:27-28. Zedekiah was taken to Babylon blinded in 586 B.C.—II Kings 25:7). Their prayers therefore became personal rather than national, and sin became a very intimate matter involving the spiritual welfare of the individual. The whole technique of religion was shifted.

30 What part did the priests have in the matter?

Cut off from their usual functions in the Temple they were probably badly confused at first. It would have been natural for them to do whatever they could to maintain some semblance of the ancient ceremonies, for that was all they knew. But in Babylonia many of them turned to literary efforts in which they elaborated the law, compiled historical records, and wrote religious tracts for the purpose of maintaining the faith of the people. They were a connecting link between the old and the new, bridging the period of transition for the people.

31 How many priests were there in Babylonia?

It is impossible to know any exact numbers, though we do know that some were included in both deportations (II Kings 24:14-15; 25:11).

32 What part did the prophets play in the transformation?

When Judah was first reduced to vassalage, Nebuchadrezzar conceived a good opinion of the prophets as a class because of the activities of Jeremiah, who had counseled acceptance of the hard terms laid down (Jeremiah 29:4-11). He believed that Judah's helplessness was such that the little nation should make the best of a bad situation and win the good will of the Babylonians.

We know that Jeremiah himself was given a large measure of freedom because of the confidence the Babylonians had in him (Jeremiah 40:1-6), and this favor was probably shown to other members of the prophetic party. This was followed by a gain in the popularity of the doctrines of Yahweh. The terrible fate that had overtaken Jerusalem was convincing evidence that the sins of the nation had at last borne fruit, and in Babylonia the people showed a willingness to listen to the preaching of the prophets which they had never evidenced in Judah. The campaign against Baal, begun by Elijah three hundred years before (876-854 B.C.), was carried to a successful conclusion in Babylonia. The Jews who returned to Palesting never returned to idolatry.

33   What part did the scholars play in the transformation?

The exiles found themselves in a land where writing was commonly practiced. Encouraged in many ways to participate in the learning of the land, patriotic and cultured Jews naturally turned to a study of their own religious literature. Their experiences had been so terrible, and the problems raised were so profound, that it was perfectly natural that the more thoughtful were driven to think their way through to some reality. The inevitable outcome was that a very great interest developed, and this in turn produced some of the most important results we find in the Old Testament. In all, at least six major aspects of the transformation are to be noted.

34   What are those six major aspects?

1. The development of the synagogue.
2. The development of the Sabbath.
3. The Law (Torah) came to a dominating position.
4. The profession of scribe arose.
5. The doctrine of the Messiah took on new importance.
6. The priestly class came into great authority, largely displacing the prophets as religious leaders of the nation.

35   What was the synagogue?

In Judah, before the Exile, the Temple in Jerusalem was the only structure used exclusively for the worship of Yahweh. Pagan worship was conducted at "high places" or open altars usually situated atop some hill. At the same "high places" Yahweh worship was sometimes conducted in a crude form, with an admixture of paganism. The reforms of Josiah, led by the prophetic party, had taken a very strong position against the conduct of any worship of Yahweh outside the Temple, but the destruction of Jerusalem and the deportation of thousands of the nation's leaders altered this case very greatly.

To the ancient Hebrew there was no distinction between sacred and secular—life was all of one piece for them. All public meetings were, in some measure, religious gatherings and all legal questions were also religious questions.

The freedom granted to the Jews by their Babylonian overlord in matters of self-government was such that it became necessary to hold some meetings for adjudicating cases, publishing announcements, etc. We know, too, that Ezekiel held some meetings in his own home whereat he instructed the people. Public meetings were first held in open courtyards, but as the colonies grew they built public buildings for their accommodation.

The exact facts concerning the development of the synagogue are not known, but it seems to have grown out of the necessity of settling questions of public interest or private dispute. At any rate we know it was a need which produced the institution. Although no sacrifices of any kind were offered in the synagogue, as had been the case in the Temple, it did become a center for the nation's religious culture.

By the time the exiles had returned to the Land of Promise (536 B.C.) an elaborate system of worship had developed inside the synagogues consisting of ministrations of the priests, reading and interpreting the Law, discourses on religious subjects by accredited teachers, religious education for young and old, and the offering of prayers of penitence for personal sins.

So firmly was the institution of the synagogue grafted on the religious system of the Jews that in Jesus' day a large number of synagogues were to be found in the city of Jerusalem itself, some of them under the very shadow of the Temple. At least one was built for the accommodation of "Freedmen" who came from Cyrene and Alexandria, unable to speak anything but Greek (Acts 6:9).

36 Who managed the synagogues?

From the beginning each seems to have been a law unto itself. Each determined its own rules, ordered its own services, and chose its own elders. In time a certain similarity of procedure developed. It is interesting to note that when Jesus returned to Nazareth with a reputation the local authorities were at liberty to ask him to speak without referring the matter to any "higher-up." It is probable that the Jewish synagogue was the most democratic religious institution in the world at that time.

37 What about the Sabbath?

The fourth commandment required the Hebrews to keep the seventh day holy unto the Lord, but for many years previous to the Exile this commandment had been almost totally ignored. There is one period in Hebrew history during which, according to some authorities, at least fifty years elapsed between Sabbaths. It may be surprising to many modern Christians to discover there was no regular observance of the Sabbath according to the commandment previous to the Exile. None of the great prophets, in listing the nation's sins, ever rebuked the people for their failure to observe the Sabbath.

38 What did the Exile do to the Sabbath?

The prophets who accompanied the Hebrew exiles into Babylonia taught the people, as had the great prophets before them, that their woes originated with their disobedience of Yahweh's laws. The crushing of Judah and the destruction of the city of Jerusalem, combined with the Exile, was all so terrible that there was a very earnest desire on the part of the Jews to know exactly what the Law was, and wherein they had failed.

For nearly a hundred years, with the exception of the brief period of the reforms under Josiah, the nation had abandoned itself to pagan worship. The prophets convinced the exiles that their unhappy state was due to that betrayal of the ancient faith; and as they sought for the secret in their disobedience, the institution of the Sabbath took on an entirely new importance, assuming an aspect that was definitely patriotic.

39 What was the connection between the Sabbath and patriotism?

Jeremiah had promised the people that they would be permitted to return to the Land of Promise (Jeremiah 29), though he assured them that the Exile was to be a long one. In spite of all their defections the ancient faith was strong within them, and the hope persisted that their nation would be restored. Consequently the belief grew up that all those who kept the Law faithfully would hasten the day of restoration; and this meant, of course, that those who observed the Sabbath were contributing to the national salvation. It was worthy as an idea, but it led to some disastrous results.

40 How could the results be disastrous?

The Sabbath commandment, in spite of the fact that it was more explicit than others, was capable of wide interpretation. The people were commanded to "keep the Sabbath Day holy" and not to profane it with any kind of work; but this still left the question open as to what "labor," "keep," and "holy" meant in exact terms.

It was agreed, for instance, that plowing was labor, but just what constituted plowing? It was perfectly obvious that turning the ground over with an iron-shod implement was plowing, but was turning the same ground over with a spade also plowing? If so, did the act of turning earth over by any means constitute plowing? Such fine points required the judgment of skilled men, and it is at this point that the scribes entered the scene. They made it their business to judge in such matters. The whole process went to such extremes that piety was in danger of being reduced to an absurdity.

41 What about the development of the Law?

When the Hebrews at the foot of Mount Sinai entered into the covenant with Yahweh whereby he was to be their God and they were to be his people, it was stipulated that they were to keep his laws. The first statement of the Law was probably very simple. But even Moses found it necessary to "interpret" the Law and apply it to specific situations (Exodus 18:13-16). Through the centuries that intervened between Moses and Babylonia the Law had been amplified by the judges, by the decrees of kings, the teachings of the prophets, and the practices of the Temple, until it was an elaborate system which had never been completely reduced to writing. The prophetic party, in writing the Book of the Law (found in the Temple in 621 B.C.), believed that they had codified this body of law in terms of the life situations of the seventh century, and that they had been true to the spirit of Moses in applying his principles as they had been amplified and applied by the prophets of the eighth century B.C.—to the new conditions under which the people had to live.

In the Exile the people became convinced that their future

rested with their faithfulness in keeping the Law, and this required an exact knowledge and a perfect understanding. Loyalty to the Law filled all the sky for the devout Jew, and the Law very logically gave rise to the profession of the scribes.

42 Who were the scribes?

In general it may be said that they were devout scholars among the exiles who gave consecrated study to the Law in an effort to define the duty of the people. At first they did their work purely as a matter of spiritual or intellectual interest, but in time they became a profession and earned their living thereby, somewhat as a modern lawyer does.

43 Were they not a superficial class?

The scribes in the New Testament, from whom most Christians derive their impressions of the class, do not show up to a very good advantage, it must be admitted. But we must also remember that originally they were devout men seriously trying to know the will and mind of God in order that they might provide the nation with safe guidance in the emergency. They thought of themselves as in the nation's first line of defense. If they did their work faithfully and well the hour of the nation's deliverance might be set forward many years. Their understanding of God may have been a mistaken one, but their motives were above suspicion

44 What about the doctrine of the Messiah?

The word "Messiah" means "anointed," as the word Christ (*Christos* in Greek) means "chosen" or "anointed," and referred to one who had been divinely set apart for a special mission. In the absence of any king the people were left without guidance except as some priest assumed responsibility. In the utter hopelessness of their conditions a hope began to develop among them that Yahweh would send them a deliverer, by whose wisdom the kingdom would be re-established and under whose leadership the nation would rise to a position of world power. Although there are hints of the germinating of the messianic idea in the eighth century (Isaiah 7-9), the doctrine did not develop in its full form until long after the Exile. But the hope which blossomed in the doctrine was a part of the religion of the exiles.

Scholars began to search the histories of the nation and retell the stories of ancient heroes. Others began studying the ancient records to discover, if possible, some clue to the nation's successes or misfortunes, and ended by pointing out that all their woes were closely linked to disobedience. All the while an intense nationalism was rising among certain groups of the people which emphasized the close connection between loyalty to Yahweh and the ancient glories of the kingdoms. Faith in Yahweh's ultimate vindication of himself kept the national spirit alive, and the doctrine of the Messiah began to develop as an integrating force which held the people together and kept them in courage through the long years of the Exile. Because of their faith in the ultimate triumph of Yahweh the zealous patriots among the people disciplined themselves and tried bravely to keep the multiplying requirements of the Law.

45 What about the priestly class?

Until the time of the discovery of the Book of the Law (621 B.C.) it was supposed that Yahweh spoke only through the voice of some living prophet. When Huldah, the prophetess, announced that the word of God was contained in the book the written word gained an authority it had never had, and men who might have turned to prophecy now turned to literature as a medium through which to express their religious convictions. This, of course, lent great emphasis to the sacred writings, and religious literature came to have a profound influence among the people.

The new place of the Law in the lives of the people, the new emphasis upon the Sabbath, the new significance of the synagogue, and the necessity of rendering a correct and proper obedience to the Law, all had the effect of investing the priests with a national and spiritual importance they had never had. This, in turn, subjected them to an unprecedented authority.

David had sensed the need for a more dignified priestly order in his day and had appointed a certain Zadok to be the royal priest (II Samuel 8:17; 15:24-36; I Kings 1:32-45), and through the years that followed his descendants rose to enjoy a status somewhat superior to that of other priests. The rich livings went to the Zadokites. The period of the Exile saw them rising still higher in the scale, and in Jesus' day no man might aspire to the high priesthood who was not a Zadokite. Thus the ruling priestly faction became an aristocracy of blood, though it must be admitted that they represented a stabilizing force of very great value during the Babylonian experience. They emerged with an authority unchallenged.

46 What literature did the Exile produce?

There was one great book produced which was called "The Book of the Kings." It appears in our Old Testament as I and II Samuel and I and II Kings. Then, in addition, there were the two books of Joshua and Judges, and at least two books of prophecy—Ezekiel and Second Isaiah (Isaiah 40-55).

47 What about "The Book of the Kings"?

When the Scriptures were translated out of the Hebrew into the Greek, about 250 B.C. (see Study No. 1 in this series), the translators found that four rolls of paper were required for a complete translation. As a matter of convenience the book was divided into four parts, approximately equal, each of which filled one roll. It will be necessary to remember that the original composition did not have any other name than "The Book of the Kings" and that the names I and II Samuel and I and II Kings were given to the four rolls, respectively, by the translators.

48 Who wrote "The Book of the Kings"?

No one person is responsible for the complete work, for the books very frankly confess of themselves that they are compilations from other and older writings. We get some identity of the compilers from the fact that they were included in a group of writings called the "Former Prophets" by the early Hebrews.

49 What writings were the "Former Prophets"?

The earliest collection of Hebrew scriptures in which these books appeared divided the prophetical works into the "Former Prophets" and the "Latter Prophets." The first group consisted of Joshua, Judges, and Kings (I and II Samuel, I and II Kings).

The second group consisted of Isaiah, Jeremiah, Ezekiel, and "the Twelve."

50 Why were the books of Samuel and Kings called "Prophets"?

They were not books of prophecy in the sense that Amos, Hosea, Isaiah, Jeremiah, Habakkuk, or Ezekiel were, for those great books consist of the sermons and memoirs of the famous Hebrew preachers. But they were prophetical books in the sense that they were compiled by members of the prophetic party for the purpose of teaching certain great convictions to which the party was committed. Whereas the "writing prophets" (Amos, Hosea, Isaiah, Micah, etc.) taught by direct means of argument and personal appeal, the prophets who compiled the Book of the Kings used history as a vehicle through which to teach the principles advocated by the prophetic party.

51 What do we mean by a compilation?

It means an assembly of material, gathered from many sources, combined to produce a more or less consecutive account. The person or persons responsible for the book's present form did not write the material, but selected it from writings already in existence, adding such statements of their own as might be required for the sake of literary unity.

52 How do we know that Samuel and Kings are compilations?

There is a very frank admission that the books have been made up from other and earlier sources (I Samuel 10:25; II Samuel 1:18; I Kings 11:41; 14:19, 29; 15:7, 23, 31; II Kings 1:18; 8:23; 10:34; 12:19; 13:8, 12; and many others). In many instances the name of the book is mentioned from which the information is drawn. In others it is possible to identify groups of material as coming from distinct sources. Nowhere does the compiler suggest that he is an eyewitness of the events described, though it is entirely possible that the original authors may have been in some instances.

53 When was the work of compilation done?

It was not all done at the same time. The first work may have been done about 610 to 600 B.C., before the Exile began, when the material in I Kings 1:1 to II Kings 23:25a was put together. I and II Samuel, with the exception of some minor additions, and the remaining portion of II Kings were compiled during the Exile, though just when the books came into their present form is not known exactly.

54 What was the purpose of the Book of the Kings?

It was the fixed belief of the prophetic party of Josiah's day (640-609 B.C.) that Judah's first duty was to obey Yahweh in accordance with the terms of the covenant of Sinai. All the true prophets believed that loyalty to Yahweh was the one sure guaranty of national salvation, and that disobedience and disloyalty were sure to result in national disaster. The first compiler of the Book of the Kings set out to write a history of the kindom for the purpose of proving that principle, and in doing so he drew on a very large amount of historical literature already in existence. But he omitted large amounts of material which would be of very great interest to us today, for in compiling his book he used only those facts which illustrated his principle or contributed to his argument.

55 What were the sources of his material?

It is impossible to identify all the books from which the facts have been drawn, but we are sure of at least three: (1) "The Acts of Solomon" (I Kings 11:41); (2) "The Book of the Chronicles of the Kings of Judah" (I Kings 14:29); (3) "The Book of the Chronicles of the Kings of Israel" (I Kings 14;19). He had access also to the Temple Records (I Kings 5-8 seems to have come from some such source), and to groups of stories about Elijah, Elisha, and the kings Ahab, Joram, and Jehu (I Kings 17 to II Kings 13). It is possible that he had in addition a biography of Isaiah.

56 What was "The Acts of Solomon"?

It is impossible to know exactly what the book was, for it has long since passed out of existence. But the compiler of the Book of the Kings chose enough from it that we know it was a more or less intimate description of Solomon and a report on his reign. Inasmuch as the prophetic party was greatly interested in centering all worship in the Temple at Jerusalem it was perfectly natural that the compiler should choose those chapters out of "The Acts of Solomon" which described the building and dedication of the sacred structure. But he also told of Solomon's sacrifices at the "high places" and his dabbling in paganism (I Kings 11:1-12). Toward the close of the story he explains the division of the kingdom on the grounds of Solomon's failure to carry out Yahweh's instructions (I Kings 11:9-13). For the most part we find the quotations from "The Acts of Solomon" in the first eleven chapters of I Kings.

57 What was "The Book of the Chronicles of the Kings of Judah"?

The varied government activities required that records should be kept of important events. As long as the united kingdom lasted these royal annals referred to the entire nation. But with the division of the kingdom each of the two resulting states kept its own annals. Therein were kept records of important events of the various reigns, it being possible to get something of an idea of the style and material recorded from various excerpts found in the Book of the Kings (I Kings 14:25-28). It is easy to identify much material from "The Book of the Chronicles of the Kings of Judah" in our book of Kings, because the compiler made his citations freely.

58 What was "The Book of the Chronicles of the Kings of Israel"?

It was the corresponding record of the kings of the northern kingdom. It will be necessary for the student to keep in mind the fact that the word "chronicles" used in the book of Kings (I Kings 14:19, 29; 16:5, 14, 20, 27; 22:39, 45; II Kings 13:8, 12; 14:15, 18, 28, and elsewhere) does not refer to the books in our Old Testament known as I and II Chronicles.

59 What were the Temple Annals?

A second record of the nation's life was kept in the Temple, for it was the center of the religious interests of the nation and, incidentally, the center also of much political interest. All large undertakings, especially wars, depended upon the Temple for blessings; the treasures taken in battle were stored in the Temple; when tribute was paid it was taken out of the Temple. The Temple Records were, therefore, reports of national events written from the standpoint of the Temple's interests.

60 Where do the Temple Records appear in Kings?

They are never mentioned, as such, by name by the compiler of the Book of the Kings, but numerous intimate and precise references having to do with Temple affairs could hardly have come from any other sources (I Kings 5-8; II Kings 11; 12:4-16; 16:10-18; 23:3 ff.).

61 What about the Elijah and Elisha stories?

About the middle of the ninth century (perhaps in its earlier years) a serious religious crisis developed in the life of Israel in which the whole system of Yahwehism was imperiled by a wave of Baalism. When the crisis was at its height a mighty prophet appeared from the region east of the Jordan who defied the popular paganism in a dramatic fashion (I Kings 17-19 and 21). Then a younger contemporary appeared to carry on the work when Elijah grew old (II Kings 2-8 and 13:14-21). About these two heroic figures a considerable number of stories clustered, and it appears that some disciple may have written them down in a permanent record. Just when this happened no one knows, but it is evident that they were available to the compiler of the Book of the Kings.

62 What about the biography of Isaiah?

We know that Isaiah did some writing himself, and that he gathered a school of disciples about him (Isaiah 8:16-20). From some of the intimate bits of information found in the Book of the Kings (II Kings 19:2, 5, 6, 20; 20:1, 4-11, 14-19) it is believed by some scholars that perhaps a brief biography of the great prophet may have been in existence, though of course the record could have been compiled from other sources.

63 Were all these books available in Babylonia?

The government and the Temple records must have been destroyed in the fire which gutted the Temple in 586 B.C., but copies, or at least large portions, were probably available to the compiler in Babylonia. But this suggests more than one compiler.

64 How could this be?

Some member of the prophetic party, believing that loyalty to Yahweh meant prosperity for the nation, began writing his history of the two kingdoms from the time of the building of the Temple down to the time of Josiah's reforms. He expected it to be a great argument for those reforms, because it would show how prosperity had attended those reigns during which the nation was obedient to Yahweh, and how misfortune had dogged the kings who had been disobedient. This history was carried off into the Exile by some member of the prophetic party, and in Babylonia, under the powerful impulse of the revived nationalism and regenerated Yahweh worship, it was enlarged and perhaps re-edited until it assumed much the form in which we have it today. By this time it may have been amplified by the addition of the great David story which appears in our Old Testament in I and II Samuel.

65 When was the Book of the Kings completed?

Some Jew living in exile in Babylonia, having the viewpoint of the prophets, took up the work where the earlier compiler had left off in 610-600 B.C., and added the last tragic record of the final collapse and destruction of Jerusalem. He gathered up the record of David's brilliant career, and probably put the entire book—I and II Samuel and I and II Kings—into much the shape we have it today. As one complete work it circulated among the exiles with very great effort.

66 How did the compiler go about his work?

We must at all times remember that he was attempting to teach religion, rather than history. He was using historical material only for the purpose of proving his case for religion. The records of the two kingdoms, from the building of the Temple in Jerusalem on down to the day in which the book was put into its final shape, were scanned for evidence of the truth of the prophetic theory. Every king was measured by two standards: (1) Was he loyal to Yahweh? and (2) Did he support Jerusalem as the one sanctuary whereat Yahweh was to be worshiped? If he met these two tests he was called "good" regardless of his political success, but if not it was said that "he did what was evil in the sight of Yahweh."

67 Did he do his work well?

In some respects he did his work so well that we are very deeply indebted to him. It is unfortunate, from our point of view, that he did not see fit to include some historical facts which might have been of very great value to us in our efforts to understand the times and their trends. We would have liked to know something about the brilliant reign of Omri, the father of Ahab, and one of the really great Hebrew kings. His rule is so spectacular in some respects that the Assyrians referred to all of Palestine as "the land of Omri"; but he is barely mentioned in the Book of the Kings, which suggests that the compiler was a Judean who did not have any interest in the fortunes of Israel. We would like to know something of the manner and life of the people, the way they lived, their social attitudes and philosophy; but this was outside the religious interest of the compiler. In spite of his bias, however, we are indebted to him for all we know of the details of those early years of Hebrew history.

68 Was his religious bias a serious fault?

The author of the Book of the Kings did not set out to write history, and the modern reader will miss the great argument of the book if he tries to read it only as history. The work presents, rather, a philosophy of history. The compiler's effort to prove his religious theory by historical data sometimes leads him into errors concerning dates, and at other times his zeal leads him to make statements that are almost fantastic, as when he says that a certain king did "that which was evil in the sight of Yahweh" (I Kings 16:19) though he reigned but seven days and probably had no opportunity to show his real character or program. This illustrates, however, the artificialty of the system used in making the record conform to a religious theory.

69 What is meant by his artificial system?

The compiler had a formula which he applied to every king.

He tells how old he was when he began to reign. He describes his reign in the light of prophetic standards, judges and weighs him, refers the reader to the sources from which he drew his information, and then passes on to the next king. The kings of Judah are all judged by their conduct in worshiping at the "high places" and the kings of Israel by their attitude toward the golden calves which Jeroboam set up at Dan and Bethel.

70 What about the David story?

If the student will make a hurried survey of the Old Testament he will discover that we have a much more elaborate account of the life and reign of David than of any other character who ever lived, previous to Jesus. Scholars are of the opinion that this is true because of the fact that the compiler was in possession of a life of David which was written in detail by someone who was an intimate of the king, and who had access to many state records and secrets.

This life of David was incorporated into the Book of the Kings by the compiler, probably with little or no change. Who the author of such a book may have been we can only guess, though it would seem quite possible that Abiathar, one of David's confidential advisers (I Samuel 22:20; 23:9; 30:7; II Samuel 15:24-29 and others), could have been the author.

The most trusted scholars in the field are generally agreed that this great David story is "the outstanding piece of prose writing and the historical masterpiece of the Old Testament." The later portions of the story, notably those dealing with David's domestic and national difficulties (II Samuel 9-20 and I Kings 1-2), come in for exceptionally high praise. The student will find it very profitable to make a special study of these chapters, reading them as the most accurate and brilliant piece of historical writing in all the Old Testament.

In the Book of the Kings we have a great work of history put together by prophetic compilers, and covering the history of the Hebrews during the entire time of their political existence as a nation. But the student must remember at all times that he is not reading pure history; he is dealing with history which is being used to prove a religious doctrine.

71 What did the Book of the King accomplish?

The Hebrews arrived in Babylon with a tolerant mind toward

the paganism with which they were surrounded. One hundred years of almost uninterrupted government-sponsored idolatry had worked serious damage to the true faith of Yahweh. Once the captives had an opportunity to get the prophet's perspective on their nation's history they began to see that their one hope lay in strict obedience to Yahweh and an undeviating observance of the Law. This was the lesson that the Book of the Kings sought to teach; and the fact that the Hebrews were well cured of their paganism when they returned to Palestine would seem to indicate that the book had very great influence upon their thinking, and doubtless played a major part in their conversion. The seduction of paganism was never again the problem after the Exile which it had been before the destruction of Jerusalem.

72 Was no new religious literature produced in Babylon?

The Book of the Kings (the four books of Samuel and Kings) consisted of earlier literature culled and compiled for the purpose of teaching a great religious lesson. The original writings from which selections were made were the product of generations previous to the Exile, but the form in which we have inherited the material is the product of the exilic activity on the part of the editor, or editors, who may have been priests or prophets. But aside from the Book of the Kings there were other compilations begun in the Exile which were completed in a later period, and of these we shall make a study in the next issue of this series. Besides these compilations, there is some Old Testament literature which owes its origin entirely to exilic writers.

73 What was that exilic literature?

In the first place, the Exile produced two great prophetic books, both of which are to be found in the Old Testament— Ezekiel and "Second Isaiah." At least two fragments which have found their way into the main body of the book of Isaiah (Isaiah 13, and 14:4-21) are believed to have been written by prophets among the exiles. But in addition the period of the Exile produced some exquisite poems.

The Hebrews were a singing people, and even so terrible an experience as the Exile was not sufficient to quench their spirit of song. Here and there, in the gatherings scattered about in Babylonia, they developed psalms which they used in their services of public worship. Like the Negro spirituals, they were composed by no one person: they were the product more likely of the political mood and spiritual genius of the people. At least one such has been preserved for us in our book of Psalms (137), and it is possible that others in our collection came into existence during the Exile but for one reason or another definite assertions are impossible. In addition to these, there is one more majestic poem found in Deuteronomy (chapter 32) which is a product of the Exile.

75 What about the thirty-second chapter of Deuteronomy?

It is known as "The Song of Moses," and many have believed it was written by Moses. But in reality it was composed by an unknown author during the Exile in Babylonia, who looked back over the history of Israel and saw the faithfulness of Yahweh standing out in marked contrast to the faithlessness of the nation. That the poem could not have come from the pen of Moses, who had but forty years' experience with the nation, is obvious. Very evidently it came from some author with a longer view of history, and such an author would have fitted perfectly into the setting of the Exile. It was written amid the enemies of Yahweh, which, again, is quite different from the setting from which Moses would have written.

76 Was it honest to use the name of Moses thus?

To write a book, or a poem, and attribute it to another person is not honest according to our standards, but in the estimation of that time it was perfectly legitimate. Literary standards were not the same then as they are in our times. The author did not use the name of Moses in order to sell his writing, nor to enhance his own reputation. He may even have had no desire to lead his readers to believe Moses had written the lines. He may have put them into Moses' speech much as a dramatist today puts speeches on the lips of famous characters of the past, as, for instance, George Washington or Abraham Lincoln. His whole concern was that the lines should be true to the spirit of Moses.

77 Was not this a dangerous precedent for scripture?

It is necessary to keep in mind the fact that *the author was not writing scripture*. Such an idea never entered his mind. Indeed, the idea of scripture was scarcely born as yet. Neither the writers of the original material, the compilers who gave us the Book of the Kings, nor the actual author of the thirty-second chapter of Deuteronomy had any idea they were writing lines which would someday serve as texts for Christian sermons. They wrote down the most profound convictions of their souls and gave their writings to their friends to read. They made no claim to any divine authority for writing (so far as any word in their books intimates), but they were content to allow their writings to stand on their own merits and maintain their own position. Because of the profound impression those writing made on later generations the religious leaders proclaimed that they were inspired. *But this claim was made for them many years after they were written, by people who had not written them, and by those who had not even lived in the same century with the authors.*

78 What about the other "Former Prophets"?

There are, among the "Former Prophets," besides the Book of the Kings (I and II Samuel and I and II Kings), two other books of historical interest—Joshua and Judges.

79 Who wrote these two books?

Like the Book of the Kings they are also compilations, made up of material written very much earlier by authors who antedated the Exile by hundreds of years in some instances. Also, like the Book of the Kings, they are called "prophetic" because they came into their present form through the literary activity of the prophetic party, and because they breathe the spirit of the great prophets.

80 Were both compiled by the same editors?

It is probable that each book represents the work of more than one writer. Both made use of the same source material, though each followed a different line, and in some instances gave a different interpretation to the material compiled. For this reason it is necessary to make a separate study of each book.

81 What was the original source material?

In Question No. 24 there was a listing of the rolls of writing which were carried away from Palestine by the Hebrews who went into Babylonia. But in addition to all those named then, there were at least two ancient historical works (perhaps combined into one) which provided the basic material for much Old Testament literature. It is impossible to go into a detailed study of these two ancient books, for it will be necessary to make such an investigation in connection with Study No. 5 of this series. For that reason we must be content with a brief statement at this point and postpone the more careful study until we approach the five books of the Old Testament known as the Pentateuch (Genesis, Exodus, Leviticus, Numbers, Deuteronomy).

82 What were the names of these ancient books?

Their authors, according to the customs of the times, gave them no names, but they are known to modern scholars as the "J" document and the "E" document.

83 What was the "J" document?

It was a very ancient book which undertook to give an account of the origins of the world, of human life, of the Hebrew race, and of the struggles of the people in establishing themselves as a free nation in the land of Palestine. It has been called the "J" document because it uses the Hebrew name YHWH for God, around which there revolves a very interesting story.

84 What about the name YHWH?

The ancient Hebrew wrote no vowels—only consonants. The divine name was spelled YHWH. The Hebrews themselves were familiar with their own words and suppled the vowel sounds when they read the written word. YHWH was pronounced *Yahweh*.

In the seventh century after Christ, Hebrew scholars, in an attempt to establish the pronunciation of Hebrew words for public reading, invented a system of vowel points, or small marks to be attached to the consonants. In doing so they assigned vowel markings to YHWH to give it the pronunciation of "Jehovah" (showing a strong Greek influence), and as such it has been translated into our modern texts, though the word "Lord" is frequently used instead.

Modern scholars, however, are using the pronunciation Yahweh more and more, and for that reason we are doing so in this study, it being the pronunciation used by those who compiled the material we are studying.

85 When was the "J" document written?

The best evidence seems to indicate that it was written about 850 B.C., in the southern kingdom of Judah, though some scholars would date it as much as fifty years earlier.

86 Who wrote the "J" document?

No one knows, though it seems to be agreed that a single author is responsible for its composition, and that he was a literary genius of the first order. The book he produced is the earliest historical record we have, and for the sake of convenience the author has been called the *Yahwist*.

87 Did the Yahwist invent his material?

By no means. He took the most authentic and trustworthy records available in his day and combined them into one great report. Even though those records were oral traditions, passed from one generation to another, they were for the most part quite reliable, and at least it can be said that there was a solid core of truth at their centers.

88 Where is the Yahwist's material to be found in the O.T.?

It forms a very large part of Genesis, Exodus, Leviticus, and Numbers, but our special interest at this moment is in those portions found in the books of Joshua and Judges.

89 How can it be identified?

The average reader must trust to the scholars at this point because he is not likely to be able to read the original Hebrew. This question, also, will be discussed in detail in Study No. 5.

90 What was the "E" document?

This was another great historical work which originated before the Exile. It was a product of the northern kingdom, and is dated about one hundred years later than "J". This makes it almost contemporaneous with Amos and Hosea. Both books had the same purpose and both relied upon the same type of material. But because "E" was an Israelite book and "J" a Judean book, we find they present somewhat different accounts of the same historical events. This fact appears conspicuously in Joshua and Judges.

91 What is the book of Joshua?

As we have already learned, the Hebrew Bible was composed of three great divisions—The Law, the Prophets, and the Writings. The Law consisted of the first five books of our Old Testament; the Prophets included twenty-one books of which Joshua was the first. It was a record of the struggles of the Hebrew people as they forced their way into the Land of Promise and established themselves as a free people.

92 Why is Joshua called a prophetic book?

The word "prophecy" has come to mean "prediction" or "foretelling" to modern Christians, but to the ancient Hebrews it means "teaching" or "exhortation." They thought of a book of prophecy as one that taught the people some lesson and exhorted them to conduct themselves in a particular way. In this sense the book of Joshua is a book of prophecy, for it is a deliberate effort to teach a great lesson, and as such was recognized by the original readers. Who the compilers may have been it is impossible to determine at this late date, though the close correspondence between the first chapter of Joshua and certain passages in Deuteronomy (1:34-39; 3:18-22; 11:22-25; 31:1-8) leads us to believe that members of the prophetic party were responsible for both.

93 How did the author proceed with his work?

The two documents, "J" and "E", had been carried into Babylonia by faithful and devout men. We can easily understand how this might happen when we think of the number of people who today carry their Bibles with them. Some scholars believe that some great literary scholar had combined the two documents into one book not long before the destruction of Jerusalem, and if this is true the combined book probably went into the Exile. At any rate, the material of the two histories was available to the compiler, who seems to have given the preference to the viewpoint of "E". Certainly the account of the conquest which we read in Joshua differs considerably from that to be found in Judges.

94 What is peculiar about the Joshua account?

The hero is a warrior named Joshua. He was one of the Hebrew leaders who came to the fore following the death of Moses. Like his great superior and predecessor, Joshua as an Old Testament figure is a little vague and shadowy. The records we have leave out many details concerning him which we would greatly like to have. Long gaps have been left in the account. In an early chapter of Exodus (17:9) he is represented as being mature enough to lead the army in battle, and in a later chapter he is described as a youth (33:11). The book of Joshua portrays him as a courageous and resourceful commander who deploys his forces with such skill that the land is overrun and subdued in two successful campaigns (Joshua 11:14 ff. and 21:43-45), whereas the book of Judges—which probably gives the more accurate account—portrays the conquest as a long-drawn-out affair in which the Hebrews are compelled to fight for every inch of territory they occupy.

95 What is the writer of Joshua trying to teach?

It was a fundamental belief of the prophetic party that Yahweh had adopted the Hebrew people and had sworn them to eternal loyalty. It had become their duty, therefore, to obey God in all matters, for which obedience they were promised prosperity and protection. The compiler of Joshua found in the story of the conquest of the Land of Promise abundant evidence of the reasonableness of his belief in Yahweh's devotion to the Hebrew people, and he told the story in a way which he hoped would arouse their enthusiasm and result in a strict obedience to his laws. Joshua is represented as delivering a farewell address to the people—a suggestion here of Washington's Farewell Address—in which he exhorts them to be loyal to the laws of Yahweh (Joshua 23). It is necessary to proceed cautiously here lest we become confused.

96 What did Joshua mean by "the law?"

To the modern man "the law of God" probably suggests a more or less vague and undetermined standard of righteousness and morality. To some it probably means the general philosophy of the Ten Commandments; but for the most part the "law" of God is an inexact and indefinite term, depending upon the interpretation of individuals. To the compiler of Joshua, however, there was nothing inexact about the Law. The Book of the Law discovered in the Temple (621 B.C.) was a precise, detailed, and explicit code. As the nation kept those laws with scrupulous care they might expect the favor of Yahweh, and as they dallied with duty they might expect misfortune. He therefore represents Joshua as exhorting the people to faithfulness and strict obedience, and in doing so appropriates the great warrior-leader and makes God the champion of the prophetic viewpoint.

97 How is Joshua appropriated?

The prophets of the Exile were intense patriots, devoted to the worship of Yahweh and the preservation of the nation. They looked forward to the day when the exiles might return to the Land of Promise and reestablish their kingdom; but this hope rested back on the idea that they must sustain their faith, their national integrity, their racial consciousness and purity, and their favorable standing with Yahweh. Life in Babylonia pressed hard against all these aims, and the people must be bulwarked against the paganism with which they were surrounded. It was not easy to obey the rules in the Book of the Law in a strange country, separated from a friendly government, and with their Temple in ruins. It was necessary to use every possible argument and reason to hold the people in line.

This was the purpose to which the story of Joshua was dedicated. The prophets sincerely believed that the Book of the Law contained the regulations of individual and national conduct of which Moses had approved, and for that reason they called them "the laws of Moses." Joshua, as the successful leader who had planned and accomplished the campaign for the conquest of the Land of Promise, was perhaps the next most influential name to which they could appeal. Just as a certain type of politician quotes George Washington as repudiating all foreign entanglements, so the prophets quoted Joshua in exhortations that the people obey the Law.

98 Is the book of Joshua not a book of history?

It uses historical material as a means by which to preach a religious and patriotic doctrine. Its primary aim is not to teach history but religion: Yahweh had come to the assistance of the people when they followed Joshua's leadership in the campaign of conquest, and would come to their assistance in Babylonia and deliver them from their captors. Using the victory of Joshua as an illustration of the way their theory would work, the prophets told the story for the purpose of strengthening the people and persuading them to loyalty in the Exile. Thus we see that the book of Joshua is not history though it is historical; it is a noble effort to present a convincing argument in favor of loyalty to the ancient covenant between the people and their God.

99 What about the book of Judges?

The second book of the "Former Prophets" is a literary product of the prophetic party as was also the book of Joshua. It was compiled by exiles in Babylonia sometime following the destruction of Jerusalem in 586 B.C., and the same material ("J" and "E", or "JE") formed its base. Its viewpoint is somewhat different from that of Joshua in certain particulars, and its record varies considerably in many details.

100 How do the two books differ?

Joshua is, in large part, the story of the exploits of one great

national hero. The book of Judges is, on the other ha
of the deeds of twelve towering figures of the period o
settlement of the Land of Promise. The title of the bo
derived from a Hebrew word which means "judges," b
whose English equivalent is "deliverers." The "judges" were,
actually, rulers with almost dictatorial powers, who reigned in
succession somewhat as kings (Judges 2:16-18).

The conspicuous difference between the two appears in the
two accounts of the conquest of the Land of Promise, Joshua
telling of a quick, easy conquest, and Judges telling of a
prolonged campaign.

There is a third difference in which Joshua represents the
nation as a more or less coherent and organized nation, moving
as a unit, while Judges tells the stories of twelve separate and
distinct tribes which moved independently for the most part
and were finally driven into a confederation for the sake of
mutual protection, much against their will.

101 How do we know the book is another compilation?

Just as in Joshua and the Pentateuch there are definite
evidences of the fact that material has been drawn from various
sources, so also in Judges we have indications that the book is
made up of selections from earlier writings. Unlike Samuel and
Kings there are no direct references to earlier volumes by name,
but by comparing two versions of the same events (the Gideon
stories—Judges 6:2-6, 11-24, 34; 8:4-21 with Judges 6:7-10, 25-32,
36-40; 7:1—8:3; 8:22-27; and the Jephthah stories—Judges 10:7,
17, 18; 11:1-11, 29, 33b; 12:1-15 with Judges 11;22-28, 30-33a,
34-40) we discover the tendency to use both versions as far as
possible. Then, in addition, as we shall find later in this study,
the book shows evidence of having been built upon an artificial
chronological framework for the sake of convenience in
reckoning. This is almost a certain mark of identification of a
compiler.

102 Who were the judges?

About two hundred years elapsed between the time of the
Exodus and the establishment of the united monarchy. During
that time the Hebrews were settling themselves in the Land of
Promise, learning the science of agriculture, fighting neighbor-

ng their gains, and growing numerous as
o national organization of any kind, the
them together being the common blood
fied them as Hebrews.

ve people need some administration of law,
here and there attracted attention by their
of character. To these, disputants brought
djudication. In such matters these leaders
civil judges. Their more important office,
however, was at of political leaders and moral guides. Two or
more of the judges may have been contemporaries, but for the
most part they ruled in succession like heads of a state.

When the Hebrews came into the Land of Promise from the
desert, they overran the country very unevenly. Some great
cities were left untouched (Judges 1:27-35), and these remained
as a disturbing element in the life of the land for many
generations. A few settlements were compact and well
defended, while others were scattered and subject to raids from
neighboring tribes. The strong person who was able to organize
defenses soon rose to a position of leadership among the
people, and in a few instances this leader was actually given the
title of "king" (9:6), though none can be said to have risen to that
dignity in fact. Indeed the compiler of Judges is very careful to
state (17:6; 18:1; 19:1; 21:25) that there was no king in Israel
during the period described.

103 What were their names?

The main narrative of the book of Judges begins with the sixth
verse of the second chapter and runs to the end of the twelfth
chapter, and in this section six judges are described: Othniel,
Ehud, Shamgar, Deborah, Gideon, Jephthah. Each of these
appears in a particular crisis and acts the hero. Five other judges
are also mentioned—Tola, Jair, Ibzan, Elon, Abdon—but very
little information is given concerning them, and for that reason
they have been called "minor judges."

104 Is the entire book concerned with these individuals?

There is one small section (chapters 17 and 18) which

describes a migration of the tribe of Dan from the south to the north and the establishment of the sanctuary of Dan. This seems to have come from some independent source, and may have been a separate piece of literary work in its original form. In addition there is a collection of Samson stories (chapters 13-16) and an episode from the history of the tribe of Benjamin (chapters 19-21), both of which may have been independent pieces of earlier literature.

105 When did these judges rule?

Roughly speaking, the Hebrews entered the Land of Promise about 1250 B.C., having left Egypt forty years earlier. The united kingdom was set up under Saul, the Benjamite, about 1050 B.C., and it was between these two dates that the judges served as leaders and rulers of the people.

106 Why is Judges called a book of prophecy?

For the same reason that Joshua was called a prophetic book—it was attempting to teach a lesson.

107 What are the five divisions of the book?

1. The introduction—1:1—2:5. This is an account of the settlement of the Land and the long struggle for a foothold. The various tribes are portrayed as moving independently and not in any concerted mass attack as is represented in Joshua.
2. The main body of the book begins with 2:6-10, which is almost a repetition of Joshua 24:28-31, and continues through to the end of chapter 12. This is the record of six crises, in each of which a judge was the hero.
3. The Samson stories (chapters 13-16), which are concerned with the Philistine crisis.
4. The Danite migration (chapters 17-18).
5. The Gibeah episode (chapters 19-21).

108 What were the six crises?

We must keep in mind the fact that the Hebrews were widely scattered over the Land, with little or no national coherence and very little national consciousness. Had they been well organized as a nation they might have been able to take the Land in a single vigorous campaign, but theirs was the weakness of divided counsels and tribal jealousies.

The six crises described in the book of Judges were, for the most part, hazards that were faced by individual tribes or sections of the nation. They may have indirectly affected the entire nation, but in comparison with modern history they were very minor, neighborhood conflicts. In terms of the life of the East, however, they were determinative of great issues. But regardless of their actual magnitude, they served the purpose of the prophets in teaching loyalty to Yahweh.

1. Othniel delivered the nation from a Mesopotamian king of uncertain identity (3:7-11).
2. Ehud, in the south, delivered Jericho from the king of Moab and drove the Moabites back across the Jordan (3:12-30).
3. Deborah and Barak, in the north, led the rural landowners and farmers in a struggle against the Canaanite landlords and city capitalists in which the fertile plain of central Palestine was thrown open for settlement (4;1—5:31).
4. Eastern tribes crossed the Jordan and began making life unendurable for the two tribes Ephraim and Manasseh, and there ensued the colorful campaign of Gideon, who was offered the title of king and refused it. His son Abimelech did attempt to reign, but his adventure ended disastrously (6:1—9:57).
5. The Ammonites, another east-Jordan tribe, took advantage of unsettled conditions among the Israelites and seized all Hebrew territory east of the river. A deliverer arose in the person of Jephthah of the tribe of Dan, who won the territory back (10:6—12:7).
6. The thirteenth chapter introduces the Philistine danger, which became a problem in Hebrew life and continued so for several centuries.

109 Is Judges then a book of history?

Though it is a book filled with historical incidents which were chosen to reinforce a religious doctrine of the prophetic party, it does at the same time give a good insight into the way in which the land was actually taken over by the Hebrews.

It was a slow process during which the original inhabitants of the land yielded one valley at a time. It is altogether unlikely that we have in Judges anything like a complete account of conquest, the silent years probably having their full quota of struggle, bloodshed, conflict, and reverses as well as victories. But the incidents recorded are probably fairly typical of the events of the entire period.

110 What was the religious doctrine of the prophets?

It was the firm conviction of the prophets in exile, which in time became the conviction of the nation, that God had been watching over the nation and that it had prospered when it was loyal to him and had suffered when it disobeyed his laws. The picture we get of Israel during the period of the judges is that of a nation constantly teetering on the edge of paganism without any great religious leader comparable to Moses. The religion of the Canaanites, with its different economic and social emphasis, was a constant temptation; and many were the lapses of which the Israelites were guilty. All these, in the opinion of the compiler of Judges, showed their effects in the misfortunes that dogged the heels of the nation. This accounts for the artificial framework of the book.

111 What about that framework?

We must remember that the book was prepared for a people living in exile under the heel of a conqueror. The destruction of their beloved capital, Jerusalem, had come as a terrible blow to thier faith as well as to their pride. With their nation broken up, their capital destroyed, and their Temple in ruins, there was a very great temptation for the people to throw everything overboard and embrace the faith of their pagan captors. But to the prophets the explanation was perfectly plain—every woe of the nation was a direct outgrowth of disobedience. When the nation remained true to Yahweh it enjoyed his blessings.

The Babylonian exile, while it was the worst disaster that had ever befallen the nation, was not the first nor the only one. In other generations the nation had sinned and had been punished for its disobedience. To the prophets nothing in all history was plainer than this fact, and they undertook to gather up the evidence to prove the case. In so doing they cast the evidence in a standard mold. Each case followed a fixed form—unfaithfulness, punishment, deliverance, peace. For each period a given number of years was assigned, and for each period there was a standard introduction: "And the people of Israel did what was evil in the sight of Yahweh, and forgetting Yahweh their God, and serving the Baalim and the Asheroth" (3:7). At the close of the report it always stated that "the land had rest" (3:11). It was an impressive marshalling of historical evidence, but not always accurate.

112 In what respect was it inaccurate?

The entire experience of the people was measured in terms of religious loyalty. No account was taken of social, political, or economic causes which may have entered into the situations. The spiritual influence of the Canaanite cities is recognized, but that the wealthy city-dwellers owned the land for which the Hebrews were contending is largely ignored. The whole interpretation of history is subject to the mold of religious dogma.

113 What did the prophets hope to accomplish with the book?

They were making every effort to appeal to the people in behalf of loyalty to the ancient faith. In the land of Babylonia, with is superior economic opportunity, education, and culture, a very powerful conviction was necessary if the people were to be held in line. The teachings of Isaiah relative to a return to the Land of Promise were sufficient to keep the flame of hope burning, but more than hope was needed if the people were to remain faithful. They must be shown that their whole national history pointed to one simple conclusion: Yahweh was not destroyed along with Jerusalem, but he was only allowing the people to undergo one more chastisement on account of their faithlessness.

114 What was actually accomplished?

It is impossible to know just how influential the book of Judges may have been in the lives of the people, but the total efforts of the priests, prophets, and religious leaders of the Jews were sufficient to turn the tide. The bitter years in Babylonia saw the Jews turn their backs upon much idolatry; and while it is true that many did lapse into paganism due to their surroundings, a purified fraction emerged from the Exile in whom there was a determined resistance to all things pagan. It is true that Jewish faith became cold and sterile, and that their ritualism degenerated into a laborious obedience to petty legal regulations largely devoid of moral significance, but in general it may be said that the nation was done with idolatry from the day of its release from Babylonia.

115 What part did the priests play in the life of the people?

Mention has already been made of the rise of the priestly class during the days of the Exile (Question 45). It is difficult, however, to reconstruct the entire picture at this late date because of the absence of details, though some few facts are well known. But to one priest, as to one prophet, we are indebted for one of the most fascinating books in all the Old Testament, and to one of his disciples, probably, for one of the most important sections of the book of Leviticus (See Study No. 5 of this series).

116 Who was this priest?

His name was Ezekiel, and he was carried away into Babylonia in the first deportation (597 B.C.).

117 What happened to Ezekiel?

Recent studies in the book of Ezekiel have raised some very interesting questions concerning the author which have not as yet been answered satisfactorily. With many of these the average person is not greatly concerned. We will then present the picture of the great priest-prophet according to the opinion generally held by the majority of careful scholars.

Ezekiel was probably a youth when the armies of Nebuchadrezzar appeared before the walls of Jerusalem for the first time. His father had been a priest before him (1:3), and probably, like Jeremiah, Ezekiel had been reared in the traditions and atmosphere of religion. Just what occurred immediately after reaching Babylonia we do not know, but when he began preaching and writing we find him in a city named Tel-abib (1:1), a considerable metropolis stretched out along the banks of the Grand Canal of Babylonia which was called Chebar.

118   Did Ezekiel know Jeremiah?

It could hardly have been possible for him to grow up as a priest in Jerusalem and know nothing of the great prophet, but there is nothing in his book to indicate that they ever met or that they ever exchanged ideas in any way. In fact, no other book in the Bible gives us any information whatever concerning the private life of Ezekiel. All we know of him is what we learn from his own writings. This is one of the strange circumstances that will be noticed in the case of almost all the prophets—they were individualists, each man working in his own way. One might be influenced by another, as in the case of Isaiah's influence over Micah, and each may have been a member of the prophetic group, but there is no direct evidence of collaboration between them.

119   What do we know about Ezekiel's private life?

Nothing in detail beyond a few simple facts. His father's name was Buzi (1:3), an active priest on duty at the Temple. This means that Ezekiel was born into the priestly class, and the fact that his father's name is mentioned indicates that he belonged to the propertied class. This was not an uncommon situation, for many of the priests were wealthy. In a later question we shall learn that he was married to a woman whom he loved very dearly (24:15-18); and it is reasonable to assume that he was a married man when he was carried off into exile, but there is no mention of any children.

120   What do we know of his life in Babylonia?

The presumption that he was a man of some wealth is supported by the fact that he lived in a furnished house of his own in Babylonia which was sufficiently large to permit him to entertain gatherings of the elders of Israel (8:1; 14:1; 20:1, 3). He was one of the leaders of the people and, though some sermons were unpopular, he seems to have exercised great influence. In contrast to Jeremiah, who suffered much at the hands of the priests and false prophets, Ezekiel appears to have enjoyed great respect. Also, in contrast to Jeremiah who never had any family of his own, Ezekiel enjoyed the comfort of a companionable woman to whom he felt himself greatly indebted.

121 When did Ezekial begin preaching?

We have no record of any activity previous to the time of the first deportation, though it is reasonable to assume that he may have been responsible for some duties about the Temple. For the first few years after the deportation he probably performed such services, as a priest, as the circumstances of the strange land would permit.

It is very easy to understand that those first years in Babylonia were difficult for a devout priest. For generations the prophets had taught the people that there was only one spot on earth whereon worship of Yahweh was acceptable—the Temple at Jerusalem. Isaiah had assured them that the Temple was the favorite dwelling place of Yahweh, and that for that reason the city would never be taken by any conqueror. Consequently it called for a severe wrenching of faith and conscience for the people to undertake any new forms of worship in Babylonia. Just as many moderns find it difficult to worship in a strange church, much more so the Jews in Babylonia found it difficult to adjust their minds to the idea of worshiping Yahweh outside of Jerusalem and the Temple. Many of them, unable to make the adjustment, sank into paganism; but those who were able to rise above the national misfortune became the nucleus of the new and regenerated nation.

Torn loose from everything he had esteemed to be religious and wrenched out of the seclusion of the Temple by the fortunes of war, Ezekiel began the moral adventure of thinking his way through these strange new conditions to a reassuring sense of Yahweh's presence, and in doing so must have lived through some very difficult hours. For five years he was at it, ministering as best he could and thinking as carefully as he was able. At last, in 593 B.C., the fifth year after he had been uprooted from his Jerusalem home so unceremoniously, he broke forth as a speaker for God (1:3).

122 What were the circumstances that prompted him to speak?

The government in Jerusalem was still intact and functioning after a fashion, though it was compelled to pay an enormous tribute each year to Babylonia. It has been weakened by the loss of thousands of craftsmen, business leaders, and capitalists carried off in the first deportation, of which Ezekiel was a part. The removal of the leading figures from the city left the rural landlords and farmers in control—the radical party of the time—ready to rise in revolt upon the least provocation. The age-old rivalry between the well-to-do city leaders and the restless rural landowners was always a menace to the peace of the land, but following the first deportation something closely resembling civil war developed. The rural landlords insisted upon an alliance with Egypt and a revolt against Babylonia, while the influential bankers and moneylenders in the capital were inclined to accept the terms of vassalage, hard as they were, in preference to the terrible vengeance they knew would fall upon them if they mutinied. The king, conceited and incompetent, favored the rural elders.

Because they were left in the land in full possession of their property, the rural landowners believed they were the favored of Yahweh (Ezekiel 11:14-21; Jeremiah 24). The deportees, on the other hand, with all the city dweller's contempt for "yokels," believed they were the ones upon whom the hand of destiny rested. Rather curiously, in spite of the harsh condemnation which Jeremiah heaped upon the government and the political leaders, the great prophet believed confidently that the hope of the nation rested with the deportees. They were the cultured, trained, and energetic class accustomed to acting as a unit, and certainly they were better informed on world conditions in general.

With the threat of complete extinction at the hands of Babylonia hanging over Judah, and with an intimate knowledge of the great striking power of the Empire, Ezekiel was convinced that the emaciated little kingdom was doomed. And in 593 B.C., in some kind of ecstatic experience, Ezekiel had a vision which became his call to prophetic activity.

123 What about that ecstatic experience?

More than any other prophet of the Old Testament, Ezekiel was subject to trances and ecstacies (8:1; 11:1; 24;1; 33:1; 37:1). Just what these experiences may have been it is impossible for us to know. There were those who, only a few years ago, believed they resembled some form of epilepsy, but that opinion is not now generally accepted. However, the priest-prophet certainly was subject to some abnormal psychic experience, and, notably, he is the only one of the prophets who seems to have been so affected. But to get anything like a comprehensive understanding of the matter it is necessary to make a more or less detailed study of these "visions."

124 What was the vision that inaugurated his call?

The circumstances seem to have made a very deep impression on Ezekiel himself, for he is careful to note the exact time—the day, month, and year—in which it occurred, a habit that characterized all his utterances. In terms of our modern calendar it was June 5, 593 B.C.

In a trance he saw a spectacle of amazing grandeur. Four living creatures and a four-wheeled chariot appeared. Above it was the crystal firmament which was the foundation of the brilliant sapphire throne on which Yahweh sat. In a great storm cloud flashing with a bewildering light it all came down from the north accompanied by a tremendous roar. The whole sight was so awful that the prophet fell down and covered his face, whereupon he heard a voice which he identified as Yahweh's, commanding him to stand up again and receive his commission (2:1, 2). This was the beginning of his spectacular career.

125 Was he always so careful about recording his visions?

Unlike most of the prophets who mentioned their visions only in passing, Ezekiel was always careful to give the exact date and circumstances surrounding his. More than any other prophet, with the possible exception of Habakkuk, Ezekiel was a writer rather than a speaker, and in his literary work he is methodical, careful, and systematic.

126 What was the meaning of this first vision?

Much time and effort has been expended by Bible interpreters in endeavors to explain the mysterious wheels, beasts, and throne. But it is dangerous to press these matters too far, for one can be misled so seriously that the central message is overlooked.

It should be remembered that Babylonia was a land where mysterious symbolism was much used. The temples were decorated with winged creatures, half human and half beast, which held various meanings for the people. Just as the eagle and the dove have figurative meanings to the American people (as also the donkey and the elephant), so these symbolic creatures conveyed some meaning to the people of Babylonia. But it is very dangerous to assign too much specific meaning to particular figures in Ezekiel's visions for the reason that they may or may not have represented those ideas to the priest-prophet.

The Hebrew Temple in Jerusalem bore no ornamentation of any kind, it being one of the laws that they should not make any graven images. The sight of such in pagan temples evidently impressed Ezekiel very deeply, and when he came out of his trances he reported his visions in terms of Babylonian images with which the people were surrounded. But there is a far deeper meaning in the vision than any mysterious symbolism of wheels, beasts, and throne.

127 What was the deep meaning of his vision?

Modern psychology explains how such a mind as that of Ezekiel would fashion its vision in terms of those figures with which he was familiar. He had doubtless visited the pagan temples, studied the symbolic creatures he saw among the decorations, and meditated on the subject at some length. Then when he came under this ecstatic spell, these pictures with which his subconscious mind was filled furnished the imagery of his visions.

But the deeper meaning is the ideas that the vision conveyed to the mind of Ezekiel, and here we are on safe ground. The vision was a call to preach; and his preaching was to emphasize (1) the supreme majesty and glory of God, (2) the fact that the presence of God was not limited to the Jerusalem Temple (else how could Ezekiel have seen God in Babylonia?), (3) God's continuing interest in the exiles in spite of their removal from the Temple and their native land. It ought to be easy to imagine the sense of relief which must have come to the prophet and the people when this truth burst in upon them that, though they might be in a strange land, they were not forgotten.

128 Why was this so important?

We can understand the importance of this concept of God which came to Ezekiel only as we investigate the common idea of all gods which prevailed in the ancient East.

According to popular theological thought each nation had a god and each god was linked with some nation. Their destinies were tied together. If a nation were destroyed it was because its god was impotent. If a nation rose to power it was because the god of that nation was more powerful than his rivals. The crushing of the little kingdom of Judah meant, to them, that Yahweh had failed.

Ezekiel's declaration that he had seen Yahweh on his throne in majesty and power meant that the crushing blow on Judah had not affected Yahweh—that he was still powerful, and to be worshiped. This was great good news to the Jews. But it also raised a problem.

129 What was the problem?

The plain Jew immediately asked, "If Yahweh allows Judah to be crushed and still lives on, what does it mean?"

130 What was the answer?

In brief, Ezekiel reasoned thus: "Yahweh is not dead, and is still interested in Judah; but Israel has sinned grievously, and must be punished. When the nation has been sufficiently chastised and when it has learned its lesson, Yahweh will then restore the people and re-establish the nation. But we must remember that all our present woes are traceable to our disobedience."

131 What did Ezekiel believe about his own ministry?

1. He believed he had been called to preach to the captives about the doom that awaited Judah and Jerusalem.
2. He expected opposition (3:8) as a natural result of his message, for he was warned in advance that the people might set their faces against him.

53

3. He was told that he would receive his messages through trances and visions (3:24-27).
4. He knew his message was to be a gloomy one, and he went about preaching it with a certain grim satisfaction. There was none of Isaiah's sense of unworthiness, nor of Jeremiah's reluctance. On one occasion he took the attitude of a pleader (18:30 ff.); but on all other occasions he was imperious, declaring that the people could "take it or leave it," for he had the assurance that he was a prophet sent from God and that he was speaking words of truth.
5. His message was sweet to him, as the scroll was sweet under his tongue (3:3), even though it was bitter to the people who so richly deserved it. It is interesting to note that the scroll to which he makes reference was a book, and in view of the new importance of the written word following the official action in which the Book of the Law was adopted, this "digesting of a book" indicates the high favor in which written literature was held.

132 Where did Ezekiel preach?

Babylonia was a land in which the science of agriculture had reached a high state of development. Canals crisscrossed the land in every direction, some of them being rather imposing waterways. Palestine, a land of hills, had known nothing of irrigation or streams, the only river in the land being the Jordan, which was not navigable. Hence, when the captives arrived in Babylonia the canals looked like rivers to them. Because there were so many, the Hebrews were deeply impressed. In their songs they spoke of "the waters of Babylon."

Not far from the city of Tel-abib, where Ezekiel lived, was the famous city of Nippur, a university center at which was to be found a magnificent library stocked with Babylonian literature of all kinds. Nippur was also the religious center for all that region; and its stately temple of En-lil, once the supreme deity of Babylonia, was the home of a numerous priesthood and the scene of elaborate ritualistic and ceremonial pageantry. The great canal of Babylonia, called Chebar, connected Tel-abib and Nippur, and upon its turgid tide many boats moved, carrying the commerce of the interior. Thus Ezekiel's ministry was performed in the midst of a busy life and under the shadow of an important cultural and educational center. All this could not have failed to make a deep impression on the exiles, and it will add a bit to our appreciation of Ezekiel to know that his ministry was performed in the very teeth of paganism.

133 What was Ezekiel's attitude toward Jerusalem?

The news that filtered through to Ezekiel from time to time convinced him that the nation was still sinful, not having learned its lesson. It was not that they were merely engaged in sinful acts of immediate significance, but that the nation had been sinful from the beginning (20:8). Hosea had taught that Yahweh loved the nation as a father loves a little child (Hosea 11:1 ff.), but Ezekiel interpreted the nation's history as one long record of rebellion. In this he was probably encouraged by those who compiled the history of the nation which is found in the book of Judges. The complete destruction of the Hebrew state of Judah, and the utter devastation of the city of Jerusalem, according to Ezekiel's thinking, was the only possible outcome that would justify Yahweh's holiness, for this was the prophet's concept of God. This message he kept repeating in one form or another clear up to the time he received the news of the final collapse of the kingdom.

134 What was Ezekiel's attitude toward the exiles?

There was a strong belief among the exiles, as well as among those left behind in Jerusalem, that their misfortune was but temporary. Prophets arose among them who promised the people that they might expect a restoration at any moment; but it will be remembered that Jeremiah wrote a letter warning them that their internment would last at least seventy years (Jeremiah 29:10), and that he was scathingly denounced by one of the prophets in exile for that reason. While Ezekiel does not seem to have set any particular date for their return, he was in agreement with Jeremiah that the Exile was to continue for a long time. He was sure the nation was a sinner, and seeing no signs of repentance he foresaw nothing but disaster. But he did believe that the hope of the nation's final restoration rested with the exiles, and instead of looking for a revival in Palestine he believed that righteousness and the favor of Yahweh resting with the exiles to whom he ministered would see them rebuilding the nation.

135   What, in Ezekiel's estimation, were Judah's sins?

They were of two classes—social and ecclesiastical. He seems to have put as much emphasis upon one as upon the other. Having been reared in the atmosphere of the Temple he was sure that their ritual was offensive, and ritual meant a very great deal to him. They had worshiped images in the secret chambers of the Temple, mixing sun worship with the worship of Yahweh, even their women joining in the widespread idolatry.

But in their social affairs they had also deserted the standards of *mishpat* (social justice). Moses' laws which aimed at protecting the rights of the poor and defenseless had been ignored. Oppression, slander, exploitation, injustices heaped upon widows and orphans, licentiousness, lawlessness, lewdness, incest, bribery, cruelty—these were common sins widely practiced throughout the nation which had made punishment inevitable (22:7 ff.).

It was not that such sins were confined to any one group. Unlike Micah, who was a spokesman for the poor rural farmers, Ezekiel assumed an attitude of impartiality. All classes alike, in his estimation, were guilty. There was a conspiracy among the professional prophets to keep silent in the face of injustices so that the people did not hear the truth. The priests themselves were guilty of actual violence; and Ezekiel, as one of them, knew whereof he spoke. Sacred things were made common; the Sabbath had been neglected; the nobility had taken the lead in exploitation and robbery because that was the tradition of their class; the people preyed upon one another; the poor were ground down to earth; and strangers in the city were imposed upon (22:23 ff.). In all the land Ezekiel knew of not one citizen of sufficient character and trustworthiness to give leadership to the forces of righteousness (20:30 f.). It is a very dark picture that Ezekiel paints of his time, but it is very probably true and correct.

136   What did Ezekiel believe about punishment for such sin?

It seemed to him the crimes of the nation cried out for

retribution (7:23; 9:9; 11:6 f; 34:1-10). Judah was worse than Israel had been, and Israel had gone down in ruin. Judah was worse even than Sodom (16:48), which had suffered a terrible fate. How then could the nation hope to escape?

But the judgment Ezekiel saw was to come at first was not designed to redeem the people—to win them back to Yahweh who loved them—but to punish them and in so doing vindicate Yahweh. In one of his visions the prophet saw an angel pass over the city marking the few pious ones who were to be saved before the fatal fire of vengeance was spread (chapter 9). In studying the whole matter over in true theological fashion Ezekiel worked out a new theory of sin and retribution in which he displayed the true prophetic instinct and rare insight into the character of God.

137 What was Ezekiel's doctrine of sin?

His constant reiteration of the charge that the nation was sinful (an indictment also rendered by the older and earlier prophets) had brought the people to the edge of despair. They decided that if they were suffering for the sins of their fathers for whom they had no responsibility, then there was no hope. A popular saying developed among them: "The fathers have eaten sour grapes, and the children's teeth are set on edge." In other words, the children are suffering for sins in which they had no part. It all seemed unfair, unjust, and utterly without hope.

To counteract this belief, and to vindicate the justice of Yahweh, Ezekiel worked out the idea that each individual is responsible for his own sins only. His statement of the case is one of the noblest in all the Old Testament: "The soul that sins shall die. The son shall not suffer for the iniquity of the father, nor the father suffer for the iniquity of the son; the righteousness of the righteous shall be upon *himself*, and the wickedness of the wicked shall be upon *himself*" (18:20). This meant that everyone would stand in the presence of God in their own right, unaffected by the sins of any other person.

But Ezekiel went even further. He delcared that no one sin would seal anyone's fate so long as there was repentance (33:11 and chapters 18 and 33). This opened wide the door of hope to the individual sinner, and represents one of the loftiest concepts to be found in all the Old Testament.

138 What authority did Ezekiel have in Babylonia?

He had no authority except that which always inheres in the office of any priest, plus that which accrues to a man of character. As he declared himself a prophet he was given also the respect that was usually tendered to one of his profession. But there was no organized religious system among the exiles which was capable of conferring any authority on him. The weight of his words and his devotion to the cause of the people were the only credentials he possessed, but his own concept of his responsibility as a pastor opened the way for him and he became the outstanding voice among the people.

139 How did he serve as pastor?

Along with Ezekiel's vision he seemed to get a sense of personal responsibility for the people and for individuals in exile. Because he saw that sin was very personal and that each man suffered for his own sins, Ezekiel felt under obligation to warn every exile. Though he lacked much of the tenderness of Hosea and the solicitude of Jeremiah, yet he does extol the office of a shepherd of souls as does no other prophet of the Old Testament. In no other book is the pastoral responsibility for the individual set forth so clearly (3:16 ff.; 33:7 ff.).

140 How did he discharge his pastoral duties?

In a unique fashion he used symbols and signs. Isaiah went through the nation for three years clad as a slave in order to warn the people against impending doom, but Ezekiel was forever resorting to strange actions and symbolic deeds as vehicles for his message. Some of these were highlighted with trances and cataleptic spells.

Immediately after seeing the first vision of which we have any record, Ezekiel seems to have gone off into some sort of trance for a period of seven days. His prostrate and inert body attracted much attention, so that when he came out of the spell and spoke, he produced a sensation among the exiles. This was but the beginning. Sign after sign followed. At one time he lay for one hundred and ninety days on his left side to symbolize the one hundred and ninety years Israel was to suffer exile. Then for forty days he lay on his right side to symbolize the years of bondage for Judah (4:4 ff.). On another occasion he weighed out tiny pieces of food to illustrate the famine that was to attend the siege of Jerusalem (4:9 ff.). Then he cut off his hair and divided it in the presence of his hearers to illustrate the different fates awaiting the inhabitants of Jerusalem (5:1 ff.). He dug his way through the wall of his home and carried his furniture out on his back to picturize the exile that was coming on the nation (12:3 ff.).

A sharp crisis was reached in his life on the occasion of the death of his wife. Jerusalem was in the last stages of the seige at the moment, and Ezekiel received a command that he was not to mourn for the loss of his companion whom he loved very dearly, because she was to be the symbol of the stricken city. When the Temple was finally destroyed, and the city of Jerusalem finally taken, it was a token that the judgment of Yahweh had fallen at last and that now the way was opened for the new and restored Israel (24:15 ff.). At times he spoke in parables—the useless vine (15), the two eagles (17), and the lion whelps (19).

141 What is the explanation of his trances?

It is impossible at this distance to know whether they were the result of some strange mental condition or were self-induced. If he was stricken with some divine power then his case is unique, for no other prophet records any such experience. If the spells were deliberately induced then they were part of a conscious effort to impress the people. The whole question has given rise to more controversy and misunderstanding than any other connected with Ezekiel. It has likewise made the book the storm center of the cults, so that it has become the happy hunting ground for all the theologians who have strange and weird doctrines to prove.

142 What can we believe about them?

Whether the man was stricken, or that he induced upon himself some sort of hypnotic spell, he came out of the experiences with definite convictions concerning God's dealing with the nations—convictions that may have formed within his mind before the trance but which, in the trance, found the vehicle for their expression. But it is important in every case to note that his visions are not his message. He made the message perfectly plain even though the imagery of the vision sounds strange to modern ears. We must not forget that Ezekiel always interpreted his own vision, telling its meaning. Without these interpretations the visions would be meaningless. To try, then, to read mysterious interpretations into them now, in support or explanation of some modern case, is to be untrue to the prophet.

143 **What did Ezekiel preach to the exiles about Jerusalem?**

After the fall of Jerusalem he no longer preached judgment but hope. He believed the exiles would be returning to the Land of Promise, and perhaps in the not far distant future (chapter 34), with the result that his message was encouraging (chapter 36). Of course, as a captive, he was not allowed to return to Jerusalem, and his reaction to the destruction of the city at the time of his wife's death indicates that he believed the capital deserved a terrible judgment. But that was only a temporary phase of his ministry.

144 **How long did Ezekiel preach against Jerusalem?**

Until the city fell in 586 B.C., or about five years. The first twenty-four chapters of his book are sermons and addresses delivered during that time.

The second period of his ministry is occupied with threats deirected at foreign nations whose sins call for punishment at the hands of Yahweh (25-32). The third period of his ministry portrays the great future for the people when the days of punishment are over (33-48).

145 **How was his message received?**

We know that the prophet Jeremiah was a victim of much opposition, and that he suffered for his temerity, but in the case of Ezekiel we hear of no such trouble. From a few words, such as "briers," "thorns," "scorpions," "rebellious house," we may infer that he met with some hostility, but there is no direct reference to such. Certainly there is no hint of direct persecution. On the other hand, on at least three occasions his advice was sought by the elders of Israel (8:1; 14:1; 20:1), which indicated they expected him to speak to them on Yahweh's behalf. But when his predictions were not immediately fulfilled the people were apt to pass him by with good-natured indifference (12:22, 27). When Zedekiah (the king who was left behind on the throne, following the first deportation) finally revolted and the vast military machine of Babylonia was set in motion to crush the little state, Ezekiel passed through one of the most bitter hours of his life. He had good reason for marking the date down, for on that day he passed through a great personal sorrow.

146 What was Ezekiel's sorrow?

His wife died and in the midst of his grief he learned that Jerusalem had fallen. She seems to have been greatly beloved by the prophet, but in obedience to the command of Yahweh he refused to mourn (24:15 ff.), as has been explained (Question 139). In this we get something of a hint of his tender nature under his stern exterior. Everything in his life was dedicated to his ministry.

147 What was the effect upon the people?

On Ezekiel the news of the fall of Jerusalem had the effect of fanning a hope into flame. But the people felt that the world had been swept out from under their feet. They had nothing left in which they could believe. The inviolability of Jerusalem was clearly untenable; Jerusalem and the Temple were in ruins; the pitiful remnant left in the land provided little assurance that the nation would survive. Babylonia, the pagan, was the undisputed conqueror of the world. It looked as if Yahweh were done for: if he could not save himself he could not save the nation. Forthwith there settled down upon the people a terrible blackness. Despair filled their souls. "Our bones are dried up, and our hope is lost," they said. "We are clean cut off" (37:11). In this extremity Ezekiel began preaching a new message.

148 What was this new message?

Instead of the old message of doom Ezekiel now preached a

message of hope. Because he believed in Yahweh he would not surrender to despair.

149 What was the basis of that hope?

From chapter 34 onward Ezekiel holds out a promise to the people that Yahweh will take special responsibility for them. Their kings and leaders had failed; their woe was a direct result of official mismanagement. The prosperous were responsible for the misery of the poor (34:18 ff.), but Yahweh is going to put an end to all such exploitation (34:11-16). The people are to have a leader who will have compassion upon the poor and weak (34:23 ff.). What a thrill this must have sent down through the ranks of the exiles! But Ezekiel was not content with promising good to God's people; he also predicted doom for their enemies.

150 Who were the enemies of the Jews?

While the Babylonians had closed in on the helpless little state of Judah, the neighboring nations had looked on with glee. The disasters were regarded as tokens of good fortune for themselves. The Edomites, especially, expected to fall heir to the land (chapter 35), and they swarmed along the border like vultures. But even more than their gloating was their sin of thinking Yahweh was important.

151 What did Ezekiel have to say?

The desecration of Yahweh's name, in Ezekiel's opinion, was atoned for in the destruction of the Hebrew state and the sufferings of the Jewish exiles. But the effrontery of the Edomites, Ammonites, Moabites, and Philistines still remained as a challenge to Yahweh. To vindicate himself he was in duty bound to visit his wrath upon them also. Therefore the prophet predicted terrible disasters for them "Then you will know that I am Yahweh" (35:9). In a series of prophecies against Ammon, Moab, Edom, and the Philistines (chapter 25), Tyre and Sidon (26-28), and Egypt (29-32), with a special word for Edom (35), Ezekiel indulges in the most vivid denunciations. These chapters show the sternness of the man. There is not one generous word in any line. It is easy to understand, for those who were left behind suffered terribly at the hands of their neighbors (25:3, 8, 12, 15). The people of Tyre expected to make money by the destruction of Jerusalem and welcomed the tragedy (26:2); Egypt had shown herself utterly untrustworthy (29:6 ff.); all were alike insufferable (28:2; 29:3).

152 Did Ezekiel see no hope for these cruel neighbors?

He was in no sense an internationalist. He had no interest in providing salvation for Judah's neighbors. He saw their gods as inferior to Yahweh; he regarded their sins with loathing and their punishment with satisfaction. The Edomites who had taken over the land were to be destroyed (chapter 35). The people who remained on the land, instead of being heirs of the hope, were murderers and idolaters and were to be destroyed (33:23-29).

153 Did Ezekiel anticipate a reform among the exiles?

The prophet says little about any sins of the exiles. The sins he condemns are the basic sins, and his interest is in their forgiveness (36:25). But he did believe the people of Yahweh were to be restored; and in a picturesque vision in which dry bones (representing the dead nation) were brought together and reanimated (37:1-14), this hope is set forth in positive terms. Even the remaining members of the northern kingdom of Israel who are faithful are to be restored (34:11), though the promise is only to the righteous (20:34-39; 34:17-22). To the remnant Yahweh is to give a new spirit—his own spirit—which is to make of them a new people (36:25-27). All this was not a reform among the Jews, but rather an evidence of the grace of God, a free gift from Yahweh who had never ceased to regard them as his own. But in Ezekiel's mind there was another reason for Yahweh's salvation.

154 What inspired Ezekiel's hope for salvation?

Ezekiel believed Yahweh would be vindicated. He did not believe such a God would allow himself to be discredited. However willing he might be to punish his people because of their agelong disobedience (20:8, 14, 21, 44) he would not do so lest at the same time he might discredit himself. For his "name's sake" Yahweh was obligated to Israel just as certainly as Israel was obligated to Yahweh. He had an obligation of honor to sustain his own name, reputation, and character. This deep and vital idea, with the sense of obligation at its center, explains one of Ezekiel's doctrines in the later years.

155 What was that later doctrine?

The complete restoration of Yahweh's good name. In order to make the name of Yahweh great, to demonstrate the greatness and power of his name and character, Ezekiel predicted that an enemy from the north—Gog of Magog—would march down like a great army; but Yahweh would fight Judah's battles and this time the victory would be so complete that it would take seven months to bury the dead and the captured weapons would serve as fuel for seven years (chapter 39). It is interesting to note that no such enemy ever appeared and the prophecy remains unfulfilled to this day, though cultists have speculated much concerning it. But even more interesting than the prophecy of the military victory was Ezekiel's prediction of the restoration of the Temple.

156 What did Ezekiel predict concerning the Temple?

As the prophet looked into the future and foresaw the vindication of Yahweh, he saw also the restoration of the Temple as a logical accompaniment. His vocation as a priest made the Temple of greater significance to him than to Isaiah, for instance. At any rate Ezekiel believed it was to be a cleansed and redeemed institution and the priests thereof were to be very select (44:9-14).

In one of his early visions Ezekiel had seen Yahweh leaving the Temple (11:23), but now he sees him returning (43:1-4). The very name of the new city is to mean "Yahweh is there" (48:35), but to make sure the holy place will never again be deserted it must be protected against profanation. Therefore the prophet presents an elaborate plan (40-48). The ritual of the restored Temple is described in great detail. The government is to be restored (he speaks of a "prince" instead of a king in order to set the fears of Babylonia at rest) and justice is to be established (45:8-12; 46:18). Here is the first declaration of the superiority of the Church over the State.

157 Was the prediction fulfilled?

When the exiles returned and began rebuilding the Temple they seem to have given little thought to Ezekiel's blueprints, and in this respect it can be said that he was ignored. Yet there is no question but that his ideas had great influence upon Haggai and Zechariah, and Ezekiel's great vision of the stream flowing out of the Temple (chapter 47) was extremely impressive in the thought of the people. The exiles did save the nation and vindicated the name of Yahweh.

158 What was the total effect of Ezekiel's ministry?

During the first years he seems to have been unpopular because of his preaching of doom, but after the fall of Jerusalem he came into high favor (33:30-33). We know nothing of his final fate, but his ideas helped fix the pattern of Jewish thought for hundreds of years afterward.

159 What was his great contribution?

He kept the torch burning as he watched Judah die, and he taught the people they could go on trusting when all the trappings of their faith were destroyed. This was a service that would entitle him to lasting honor. His emphasis upon personal responsibility, with each man responsible for his own acts, sins, and soul, set a new spiritual standard.

His emphasis upon the majesty of God, upon his international authority, his superiority to all other gods, was a long step in the direction of monotheism, though he cannot be credited with establishing that idea. But it is important that he insisted upon the supremacy of the spiritual over the political, of the Church over the State.

His strong insistence upon the importance of ritual paved the way for the development of the rigid legalistic system of later years, which had so much to do with making Judaism what it became. Only a strong man, unrelenting and uncompromising, could have held the fragile community together.

160 What were his weaknesses?

Although he was capable of a great love (11:13; 24:16), there is little love in his book. He took a narrow view of his enemies and was without international outlook. He was more concerned about the majesty of God than the problems of men.

161 **What is Ezekiel's worth for our day?**

The great message of the prophet for our day is his doctrine of individual responsibility. His assurance that the sinful man may repent and enjoy the favor of God is one of the most blessed hopes we have. In spite of his theological mind, his evangelism is magnificent (33:10-11).

We must remember that Ezekiel was a product of a stern and ruthless day. He preached to a people who were face to face with death. Everything they had believed in was in dire jeopardy, and Ezekiel became the rock upon which their faith finally rested. He was convinced that the forces of right would ultimately prevail (chapters 38 and 39), and that evil was doomed.

162 **Was Ezekiel the only prophet of the Exile?**

There were several others, but, strange to say, we do not know the names of any, though we have some of their works.

163 **Where are their works to be found?**

According to the opinions of good scholars three prophetical works are to be found in the book of Isaiah, in addition to the writings of Isaiah himself. Number 1 is in Isaiah 13:1—14:23. Number 2 is in chapters 40-55, and Number 3 includes chapters 56-66.

164 **Is the book of Isaiah a compilation?**

It cannot be called a compilation as the Book of the Kings was a compilation. Rather it is a collection of prophecies.

165 **Did Isaiah not write the entire book?**

Scholars have concluded that he did not, for the very good reason that political situations are mentioned in the late chapters which did not exist until more than a hundred years after he died.

166   How did these writings get into the book?

The original copies of all prophetical writings were private property, with which the owners were at liberty to do as they pleased. They had not yet been called scripture, and no sanctity was attached to them except that which they inspired. Editors of hymnbooks of today, for instance, do not hesitate to change a line in a hymn if they think they can improve it, and in some such way the ancients regarded the scripture books until they were definitely classified as "inspired scripture," which did not come until hundreds of years later in some cases. Since writing material was very scarce it was perfectly natural that someone owning a copy of Isaiah's original work written on a roll, a part of which was blank, should hire some scribe to write the words of another prophet into the blank space. The next owner of the roll might think the entire writing was by the same author, and when he had it copied would have it done as one book. It was all perfectly natural, perfectly honest, and in time became very confusing.

167   Who wrote these additional books?

No one knows at this date, but scholars call the author of chapters 40-55 "Deutero-Isaiah" or "Second Isaiah," and the author of chapters 56-66 "Trito-Isaiah" or "Third Isaiah."

168   What about "Trito-Isaiah"?

He was a prophet who wrote in a later period, and we must delay our study of his writing until a subsequent study.

169   What about "Deutero-Isaiah"?

In chapters 40-55 we have the writings of one of the greatest of all the Old Testament thinkers, who wrote during the late years of the Exile, in Babylonia.

170   What was the state of affairs among the exiles?

It was only natural that they should look back to the days of their residence in Judea with great longing. But it must also be remembered that fifty years after the deportation there were very few left of the original deportees, and the Jews then living had nearly all been born in Babylonia. Their knowledge of the land of Judah was only hearsay, and such pictures as they carried in their minds were idealizations—the product of love and memory.

For ten years after Ezekiel's last recorded prophecy (571 B.C., Ezekiel 29:17) nothing happened to give the Jews any reason to believe their hopes of a restoration would be realized. Then, after a decade, their blinded king Jehoiachin was liberated, and a great wave of joy mingled with hope swept through the colonies of the captives (Jeremiah 52:31).

In 553 B.C. Cyrus made himself king of Persia and in 547 B.C. took the important city of Sardis, capital of Lydia. In 546 B.C. he set a Persian governor over the city of Uruk, which overlooked the domain of Babylonia. With each succeeding victory of Cyrus the hopes of the Jews rose higher. In 539 B.C. he struck against the city of Babylon itself.

This sudden turn of affairs set the Jewish communities in Babylonia seething with excitement. In the victory of Cyrus they saw the hope of their own restoration, and in this they were encouraged by various leaders. Then in 539 B.C., with the aid of some disaffected elements inside the capital itself, Cyrus took the city and the great Babylonian Empire was at an end.

171 When was Second Isaiah written?

The actual date cannot be determined with absolute accuracy, but we know the prophet speaks of the victory of Cyrus as still in the future (Isaiah 44:28; 45:1). He caught the attention of the world and aroused the hopes of the Jews in 546 B.C., and took the city of Babylon in 539 B.C. Evidently the book was written sometime between these two dates. There is every indication the writer was confident of the city's overthrow, and such confidence would be strongest just before the blow was struck. By that reasoning, then, it must have been about 540 B.C. that the prophet wrote his sermons.

172 Where did the prophet live?

Because of the fact that he is addressing the exiles in Babylonia it would be natural to infer that he was a resident of the land and one of the exiles. But chapters 49-55 reflect a Palestinian background, and there are those who believe he may have moved back and forth between Babylonia and Palestine.

173 Who was Second Isaiah?

There is nothing in the chapters to enable us to answer this question. No wife, child, or relative is mentioned. One brief passage (50:4-9) may be biographical, but does not lead to any identity.

174 What were the economic conditions of the time?

Earlier in this study it was stated that the Jews came in time to enjoy much liberty in Babylonia, and this was true. But to zealous patriots any restriction is burdensome. They were not free to move about as they pleased (45:13). When the time came for them actually to start home (recorded in Ezra and Nehemiah) many preferred to stay in Babylonia. In Jesus' day it is said that there were more Jews in Babylon than in Jerusalem.

In Second Isaiah's day the Jews were a humiliated and restless people. Babylonia was showing them little mercy (47:6); they were imposed upon (42:22); their king had been imprisoned for thirty-seven years (II Kings 25:27). The general attitude of the country seems to have been hostile, and at least two Jewish agitators had been severely dealt with (Jeremiah 29:22). Many of the exiles were skilled laborers, and they came into competition with native laborers, so that the prophet spoke of the natives as "all who are incensed against you" (Isaiah 41:11; 54:15). The exiles lived in constant fear (51:13).

175 What was their social condition?

They were aliens and competitors in the labor market. As captives they had to be content with any living conditions they could make for themselves under the eye of the government. They were held in contempt by the native population (51:7; 41:14), trampled upon (51:23), and suffered so much that Second Isaiah needed the tenderest words in speaking to them (41:17). The fact that they were able to survive is an evidence of great spiritual vitality.

176 What was their religious situation?

Their Temple was in ruins, their priests scattered, their

worship disorganized, their God despised and ridiculed throughout the East. As a result, many of them had lost faith in Yahweh. They felt that he had cast them off entirely (40:27) and forgotten them (49:14). They were like children whose mother had been divorced and they had been sold to their Father's creditors (50:1). The most bitter declared Yahweh was worn out (40:28) and unequal to the demands of the "new times" (50:2). Some were angry with him (45:24), defiant (45:9), and deliberately disobedient (48:4).

177 Did they see no hope?

Jews who were only lukewarm in their loyalties swarmed about the altars of Bel and Nebo. Images were to be found occasionally in Jewish homes (44:17). From the attacks Second Isaiah made on this subject we may judge it was more or less common. There was danger that the nation would lose its ancient faith and be absorbed into the surrounding paganism.

178 What saved them?

It is just here that we come upon one of the most interesting aspects of the work of the prophets. The northern kingdom of Israel, taken captive by Assyria, had faced the same situation more than a century and a half earlier. It surrendered to the paganism about it and passed out of existence, because no virile religious leadership existed inside the nation. Decay had set in long before the political collapse came.

In the case of Judah, however, the nation had enjoyed the ministry of at least four great preachers. Jeremiah saturated the nation with a great spiritual hope which Babylonia could not quench (627 B.C.). He was supported by the ministry of Zephaniah, who had preceded him (630 B.C.). Habakkuk exalted the power of righteousness to sustain the nation (597 B.C.). Then came the prophet-priest Ezekiel with his sublime vision and practical mind. Forty-six years after the wrecking of Jerusalem, Second Isaiah, preaching to the exiles, had the convictions of these to provide him with a background. In all the years of Babylonian captivity there seems to have been at least one voice speaking for God among the exiles, *and this saved the nation.*

179 What was Second Isaiah's message?

Above all, the prophet saw the nation in need of comfort. He knew their sinning full well, but he also knew their suffering; he had lived with them; he had shared their woes. And now, in language that still moves us with its tenderness, he sings of comfort and consolation (40:1-2)—so much so that his texts are used to this day by some of our greatest musicians as anchors for their haunting melodies. The theme of reassurance runs through all his writings.

180 Did he foresee the restoration?

It was all so real to him that he sang of it as if it were already accomplished. People in the desert are preparing a highway across which the Lord will lead his people on their homeward march (40:3-5). It is to be a smooth way, easy underfoot, and pleasant. His mind raced on ahead of the pilgrims and announced their coming to the city of Jerusalem. Yahweh had vindicated himself. With infinite care he was providing for the sick, the weak, the helpless, and the needy (40:9-11).

181 How was the message received?

To the great mass of the exiles Babylonia appeared too powerful to be overcome. Its highways were full of soldiers; its walls were impregnable; its supplies exhaustless. Answering these doubtful ones the prophet declares that all this was but grass that "withers" in the presence of Yahweh (40:6-8). Nothing could stay God's hand, for it was the mightiest power on earth, and his will was to be done (50:10 ff.). He pointed to the forces of nature, directly by Yahweh, and called the designs of people "dust on the scales." Strong nations were as nothing before Yahweh. Nothing in all the earth compares with Yahweh, either in might or mercy (40:12-17, 25 ff.).

182 What about the idols?

He dared the idolatrous nations to await the judgments of Yahweh. He challenged them to show their wisdom. With fine scorn he ridiculed the idols that were made by people's hands and had to be held together with nails (40:18 ff.; 41:21 ff.). "Compare them if you can with a great God like Yahweh," he cried. Over and over again the theme appears—"I, I am Yahweh; and besides me there is no savior" (43:11; 44:24; 45:6,

18, 21; 46:9). There could be no sharing of honors between Yahweh and any other deity (42:8). Fancy praying to a wooden image (44:17)! Certainly such small divinities could not control history (41:21). The day would come when they would be carted off like rubbish even from Babylon (46:1 ff.), the great gods Bel and Nebo going down like them all with a mighty crash. Even their fortunetelling and stargazing was folly and futility (47:12 ff.).

183   What did all this mean?

It indicates in the first place the extent to which idolatry had been making inroads into the religious life of the people. But more, it indicates that Second Isaiah had a very lofty concept of God. He saw that Yahweh was the one great God of all the world who used people and nations in working out the will of God (45:9-13). He took the long-range view of history and saw that even evil forces had been turned to good account in other days and that mighty conquerors had been as tools in Yahweh's hands. This idea of one God, mighty and supreme, unassailable and beyond the power of people to change, was the central idea of his whole religious philosophy. It was not that he made Yahweh greater than all other gods, but that he denied any other gods had any existence at all. Not even Jeremiah had come out this far in his religious thinking. He may have hoped it was true, and he may have had fleeting glimpses of the idea, but he never expressed the conviction as did Second Isaiah (44:8).

184   What was the use if Yahweh had cut them off?

This is the glory of his message. Yahweh had not cut them off: Yahweh still loved them!

185   What did he have to say about Yahweh's love for the Jews?

He admitted very frankly that Yahweh had been angry with the nation and had delivered it into the hands of Babylonia because the people were sinful, just as in other days he had allowed Egypt and Assyria to oppress them (52:4). There could be no disguising the fact: it was for their sins that they had suffered (43:27 ff.; 48:1 ff.). But they had now suffered enough and were to be comforted (40:2). This is the message to which he returned again and again (44:22; 48:9; 51:22; 54:6 ff.). He does not call them to repentance as did Jeremiah and Ezekiel, for he seems to believe Yahweh has already forgiven them. Their misery had touched his heart and worked the miracle (40:27-31). Jerusalem had paid the price of her sins twice over (40:2). Babylonia had gone too far (47:6), and Yahweh was unwilling to allow her cruelty to continue.

186 What does this indicate of the prophet's personal character?

He must have been a very kindly man, with a heart deeply touched by the sufferings of the people. There was no sternness in his message, and in all the Old Testament he is more nearly the evangel of love than any other. In no sermon is there any word of harshness or bitter rebuke for the harassed and suffering people. Over and over again he reports Yahweh as using endearing names for Israel (44:1, 21; 51:4-16); and the names he uses for Yahweh were endearing terms—"your Redeemer" (41:14; 44:24; 47:4; 54:5), "your God" (41:10; 43:3), "the Holy One of Israel" (41:14; 45:11; 47:4; 54:5), "your Savior" (43:3; 49:26), "your Maker" (45:11; 51:13; 54:5), "he who formed you" (43:1; 44:24), "your husband" (54:5). He assured them they were to Yahweh as God's own children, cared for from birth (46:3 ff.; 49:15), and therefore Israel must never fear (41:10). His mission was to hearten and comfort the people, and he performed this mission so magnificently that even down to our day his messages turn the heart of the discouraged and tempted to the heart of God.

187 Was this a new message?

Not exactly. Hosea had assured the people that God loved them as a devoted husband loves an erring wife. But it remained for the prophet of the Exile to put the doctrine into its most beautiful terms. He compared the love of God to that of a mother who has been bereaved of her children (49:16-21) and who is to be comforted with many more when the exiles return. In one instance Israel is portrayed as the wife of Yahweh (54:4-8), whom he had loved with all the eagerness of youth and whom he certainly will not cast off. In another passage Yahweh appears as a good shepherd gathering his lambs to his bosom (40:11). He will provide fresh water for them in the heights as well as in the valleys, and grow trees for their comfort (41:17 ff.; 44:3; 49:9 ff.). He will lead the blind along (42:16), loose the prisoners (49:9), help his people, (41:10, 14), and bring them safely through every danger (43:2), triumphing over their enemies (41:11, 15). Best of all, God's favor will never again be lost to them (54:10). And for their immediate needs he gave them a great promise.

188   What immediate promise did he give them?

On other occasions Yahweh had shown favor to the nation, for example bringing them out of Egypt. But the things he would do now were to be greater (43:19; 48:6; 51:9 ff.). The exiles were to be released! This seemed too good to be true, for Babylonia was mistress of all the world (49:24 ff.). But the prophet assured them it was to be so. Cyrus was to be the means by which the great deliverance was to come (45:1 ff.). He would completely overwhelm the Empire and wreak Yahweh's wrath upon it (47:1 ff.; 43:14; 46:1; 48:14). He would then let the people go free to return to their beloved Judah (45:13), leaving the loathsome scenes of their captivity behind them (48:20; 52:11 ff.). It was to be a great victory for Yahweh as well as for Cyrus, and the new monarch would recognize his indebtedness to Yahweh by sending the sacred vessels of the Temple home to Jerusalem in honor. The city of Jerusalem was to rise from the ruins (44:26), together with the other ravaged cities of the realm, and the Temple would stand again upon new and more glorious foundations (54:11). The prophet seems to have believed that Cyrus would do all this on his own initiative, as an offering to Yahweh (45:13).

189   Did the prophet believe Cyrus would worship Yahweh?

This is one of the most difficult questions in all the prophet's theology. There is no doubt but that he believed that Yahweh was the one God, and that in time all nations would come to worship Yahweh (45:22 ff.). This world-wide character of Yahweh worship was one of his great ideas, but he also believed people would come into this relationship one by one, rather than by any mass movement (44:5). Nevertheless he did believe that Israel had a peculiar mission to perform as the servant of Yahweh.

190 What is meant by the servant of Yahweh?

This is one of the most disputed passages of the Old Testament. The "servant" passages of Second Isaiah have probably been subjected to closer scrutiny than any other chapters in all the Hebrew prophets, but a careful comparison of the opinions of many scholars leads this writer to believe the most logical interpretation is that in them we have a description of Israel's sufferings in the performance of her mission.

191 What is Israel's mission?

According to Second Isaiah, Yahweh is the creator of all the world, the master of all, the ruler of all nations. At the time of writing these poems (42:1-4; 49:1-6; 52:1-15) the nation was crushed and helpless, despised by all, an exile, without any national existence, and in an utterly hopeless state; but still it was a servant of Yahweh, and destined to accomplish Yahweh's purposes. Though it may seem incredible, this prostrate nation is to be the agent through whom true religion is to be established throughout the world. The suffering through which the people are passing is part of the plan, and even though the reason for the suffering cannot be explained it is to be accepted as from God. Israel in time is to be exalted (41:15); its foes are to be humbled (41:11) and rendered powerless (54:15). Aliens will never again profane the Holy City and its Temple (49:17; 52:1). All creation is to acknowledge Israel's position (52:10) and that it wields a sovereignty that is world-wide (54:3).

192 Is this purely nationalistic?

By no means. The nation is to be used in behalf of all the nations of the earth (42:1 ff.). It is to be a universal mission in which the love of God for all is to be proclaimed. Wherever people are suffering or oppressed they are to be told that Yahweh is their friend (42:7). Justice and truth are to be established (42:3, 4). The needy are to be assisted (49:10).

The nation is not to go out with arms or military might, but as a servant going about tasks in humility and kindness. The servant might encounter hostility, but would go on loving the world in spite of the fact that it resists the truth. The servant would suffer indignities without complaint for the sake of winning (50:5, 6). This was not to indicate weakness, for the servant would walk in the courage of Yahweh (42:4; 50:7). The picture of the conquest is contained in the matchless fifty-third chapter, which is, in the opinion of many, the most beautiful single chapter in the Old Testament.

194 What is the fifty-third chapter of Isaiah?

It is a great poem descriptive of the suffering servant.
1. Yahweh calls upon all the nations of the world to consider the case of Israel (52:13-15).
2. The heathen nations speak (53:1-3).
3. Now they see that the servant has suffered for them and they confess their sins (53:4-6).
4. The prophet agrees with them and describes the suffering of the servant and his patience (53:7-9).
5. This is all a part of Yahweh's plan, without which there is no hope of religion ever reaching the heathen in its true form (53:10-12).

195 Is this a prediction of Jesus?

Many Bible teachers have referred to it as such, but we must be careful to keep step with the facts. The prophet identifies Israel, the nation, as the suffering servant (41:8; 49:3). When he speaks of an individual it is a personification of the nation, just as we sometimes speak of truth and say, " 'Her' banners shall never trail in the dust."

It is a fact, of course, that Jesus' life corresponds very closely to the prophet's portrait of the suffering servant. More than any other person who has ever lived Jesus fulfills the conditions. But the fact that Jesus fits into the picture does not prove that the prophet was predicting Jesus. It is undoubtedly true that, as Jesus meditated upon this great passage, its idealism affected him very deeply. The idea of vicarious suffering—one suffering for many—which is the great characteristic in Jesus' life and work, roots back in this picture of the suffering servant. Since the prophet actually names Israel as the suffering servant, it would hardly be accurate to say he was predicting another. It is certainly true that Jesus was *a* suffering servant, but Israel seems to be *the* suffering servant the prophet had in mind. However, Jesus took up in his own person all the qualities and character of *the* suffering servant Second Isaiah described, and in that sense may be called by that beautiful name. The important thing to notice in these passages is that both Israel and Jesus embody the same great spiritual principles and purposes, and both suffer because of the evil-doing of others.

196 What was that great spiritual purpose?

It was the belief of Second Isaiah that Yahweh did not plan to glorify Israel for her own sake, but for the sake of the whole world. The servant is not suffering for himself, but for all people as sinners. Yahweh, he believed, is seeking to win all nations to himself, and in seeking them is using the suffering servant. Therefore the servant is to bring all men to acknowledge and worship Yahweh (49:5). Here is the great evangelistic message of the Old Testament. No other prophet has any such view of world destiny and work. None other has the same passion for redemption.

197 How is Israel to do this work?

Certainly not by military might, but by a divine power which will be given to it as it undertakes to perform its holy commission. The people of the world will recognize Israel as the messenger of Yahweh, the true God (42:1-4), by the fact that it suffers vicariously for all the other nations.

198 What does the prophet mean by true religion?

He has a very definite idea of personal religion, but he also thinks of religion in terms of justice (42:4). Just as Amos placed the emphasis on social justice rather than on ritual and ceremony, so also does Second Isaiah. Nowhere in his book does he argue for any of the forms of religion. This is rather strange, for he was preaching in a day when the purified and spiritualized ritual was coming into high favor, due to the influence of Ezekiel. He has little or nothing to say about the Law or the priesthood. He lays no emphasis on the Temple or the ordinances of the altar. Religion to him is social justice, right human relationships, and the assurance and comfort of Yahweh.

199 Did Israel fulfill his hopes?

Without question the prophet idealized the virtues and righteousness of the nation. In actual life they were no such holy people as he described. But he was attempting to portray the ideal rather than the real. He knew as a matter of fact that a nation composed of people who had been robbed, plundered, exploited, and imprisoned (42:18-22) was not holy and purely spiritual. They had rebelled all their lives against these harsh conditions. They had no such divine concept of their mission as the poet-prophet had, and he was trying to impart to them such an understanding of their hardships as would glorify their sufferings and give them courage. He was attempting to arouse them to a great life by holding up before them a great concept of their mission.

200 Why is Second Isaiah called a poet?

Because the entire section of Isaiah which is credited to him is written in poetical form with the possible exception of one small section (44:9-20). Many scholars now believe that, while this passage is not as rhythmic as the rest of Second Isaiah, it too should be rendered in poetic form. The original and historic Isaiah, whose writings comprise the first chapters of the book, was not a poet, though many of his lines are as beautiful as any poetry.

201 Does the prophet take high rank as a poet?

In some of his passages he rises to great heights and becomes the supreme comforter of the Old Testament. Superb in his passionate love for the nation, overpowering in some of his descriptions of the majesty of God, tender in his compassion for the suffering exiles, clear and logical in his reasoning, and always winsome and kindly, Second Isaiah will take rank as a preacher with Isaiah or Jeremiah, and as a poet will rank with the best the Hebrews produced. There are many who find in him the greatest soul of them all. But it was his doctrine of vicarious suffering which marked him as unique among the Hebrew prophets.

202 What was this doctrine of vicarious suffering?

All the other prophets—Jeremiah, Isaiah, Zephaniah, Ezekiel—believed the Children of Israel were suffering for their sins. Second Isaiah believed they were suffering for the sins of others, and that through their suffering the world was to be redeemed. Therefore he called upon them to be patient for the world's sake. This was an entirely new note in religion, and of course as Christians we believe it reached its sublime and complete expression in Jesus of Nazareth. It is for this reason that so many people have been ready to believe the "servant passages" were predictions of Jesus. But as we take the long-range view of the history of the Jews, and see how the faith did develop through suffering, we can understand why the prophet was justified in thinking of the nation as the suffering servant of Yahweh.

203 What was the prophet's great contribution to religion?

The prophet was an enthusiastic soul and he occasionally idealized his picture a bit. Israel was never so lofty a people as he described them as being. Nor were his predictions about Jerusalem all fulfilled. But he has given us a majestic concept of the greatness of God, and of the holiness and love which characterized God. God has not gone off and left the world, but is at grips with its problems and is in the act of redeeming it. God is not a God of the past, but of the present and the future. It is very significant that when Jesus stood up in the synagogue in his old home town to read the scripture and explain his mission to his former friends and neighbors, he took a text from the writings of a pupil of Second Isaiah's (61:1 ff.) as the basis of his lesson. As one writer has described it, the prophet's doctrine of vicarious suffering is "the deepest place in all the ocean of the Old Testament."